D1073252

My FOUR GRANDPARENTS

Chronicles of DeSoto Parish Louisiana

JEROME F. WHITE

My FOUR GRANDPARENTS

Chronicles of DeSoto Parish Louisiana

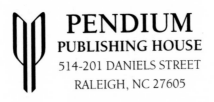

PENDIUM
PUBLISHING HOUSE
514-201 DANIELS STREET
RALEIGH, NC 27605

For information, please visit our Web site at
www.pendiumpublishing.com

PENDIUM Publishing and its logo
are registered trademarks.

My Four Grandparents
by Jerome F. White

Copyright © Jerome F. White, 2017
All Rights Reserved.

ISBN: 978-1-944348-21-2

Dedications

I dedicate this book to my ancestors, family, and friends:

Jeremiah Jobe White Sr.
Ella Deloise Green White
Babe Armon Stansberry
Hezekiah White III
Dorothy White
Lugene Green
Sandra Oten
Velberly Nelson Rodriquez
Zina Stephanie White
Jered Fitzgerald White
Jonathan Josiah White

CONTENTS

Introduction

Family is the key to all our existence. Without family, who can we count on and where would we be? This book is representative of over two hundred years of American experiences originally tied to South Carolina, Georgia, and Alabama, but all ends up in DeSoto Parish, Louisiana.

This journey has been documented to give America a perspective regarding the southern United States generally, and northern Louisiana specifically. This book is not tied to the Creole people of southern Louisiana. Louisiana is internationally known for the historic French Quarter, as the birth place of jazz and its Creole and Cajun cuisine, but these affiliations are not relevant with this story. The assimilation of cultures between my four grandparents and the French and Franco-African connection are not applicable. In addition, this journey is not tied to the Spanish settlers of Louisiana. Very few names have been changed. This book is not designed to protect the innocent. There are no innocent; just experiences explained to capture an era, to tell it like it is, or how it was seen through the eyes, views, readings, stories told, actual experiences seen and the spirit of the African American people. This book recounts experiences that honor a segment of America not commonly praised. It is time to give honor to a people well deserving of acclamation.

Even if you are a minority of one, the truth is the truth

Mahatma Gandhi
(Alkire & Newell, 146)

Family & Politics

Mahatma Gandhi said, "What is truth? A difficult question; but I have solved it for myself by saying that it is what the 'Voice within' tells you" (Hick, et al., 99). America is the greatest country in the world; therefore, its democracy is elastic enough to attempt to do better when a problem is identified. Slavery was legal in America at one time but does not exist today. At one time in America woman couldn't vote but today women are given that right. Although change may take time, America's democracy is flexible in adjusting legislatively for what is right. It must be mentioned also that sometimes change in America has come at the expense of the blood, sweat, and tears of brave individuals.

I have conducted an intricate analysis of the history of my four grandparents. It is interesting to know that each of the four grandparents were themselves only two generations away from slavery. The unfair share cropping system was pivotal in inspiring the family to have financial independence. Farming and agriculture was a way of life and vitally important to the American economy. The separate but equal doctrine was at its peak during the prime of their lives. They all survived the great depression. The following chart shows the political parties of the four grandparents in both 19th and 20th century America:

Table 1
Political Party Affiliation

Number	Description	Erma Freeman	Willie Green	Senie Winters	Jesse White
1	Political Party	Democrat	Democrat	Democrat	Democrat
2	Paternal Political Party	Democrat	Democrat	Democrat	Republican
3	Maternal Political Party	Democrat	Democrat	Democrat	Democrat

Note that these four grandparents, in addition to their parents, were Democrats with the exception of Jesse White's father, whose name was Hezekiah White Sr. A successful business man, Hezekiah White Sr. was a Republican. As was the case with most blacks after the civil war, he chose to be Republican primarily because Abraham Lincoln was affiliated with the Republican Party. They seemed to be thinking, "If it is good enough for Honest Abe, it is good enough for me."

George Santayana said, "Those who cannot remember the past are condemned to repeat it". Sometimes the best indicator of the future is to look back at our past. Reflection has its purpose. The President of the United States is the single most powerful person within our American democracy. With that said, one doesn't have to look solely at a very important person (VIP) in our United States history books to understand the true impact of various laws. One can even look at American history from the perspective of how did it affect one's own bloodline. Presidential decisions impact everyone within our nation. It is only appropriate to bring attention to the most powerful men in charge whom affected these four grandparents life. During the life spans of Erma Freeman, Willie Green, Senie Winters, and Jesse White, the following United States Presidents were in office:

Table 2

Presidents in the Lifetimes of My Four Grandparents

President Name	Term of Office	Party
Theodore Roosevelt	September 14, 1901 to March 4, 1909	Republican
William Howard Taft	March 4, 1909 to March 4, 1913	Republican
Woodrow Wilson	March 4, 1913 to March 4, 1921	Democratic
Warren G. Harding	March 4, 1921 to August 2, 1923	Republican
Calvin Coolidge	August 2, 1923 to March 4, 1929	Republican
Herbert Hoover	March 4, 1929 to March 4, 1933	Republican
Franklin D. Roosevelt	March 4, 1933 to April 12, 1945	Democratic
Harry S. Truman	April 12, 1945 to January 20, 1953	Democratic
Dwight D. Eisenhower	January 20, 1953 to January 20, 1961	Republican
John F. Kennedy	January 20, 1961 to November 22, 1963	Democratic
Lyndon B. Johnson	November 22, 1963 to January 20, 1969	Democratic
Richard Nixon	January 20, 1969 to August 9, 1974	Republican
Gerald Ford	August 9, 1974 to January 20, 1977	Republican
Jimmy Carter	January 20, 1977 to January 20, 1981	Democratic
Ronald Reagan	January 20, 1981 to January 20, 1989	Republican
George H. W. Bush	January 20, 1989 to January 20, 1993	Republican
Bill Clinton	January 20, 1993 to January 20, 2001	Democratic

Whether one believes the federal government should be deeply involved with running the country or should only be involved with the infrastructure of the country, consider this one truth:

> *Our primary objective should not be to solve the problems of the universe, world, nation, and states. Our primary objective should be to work on the problems within our home (our family). If this objective is carried out, the problems of the universe, world, nation, and states will work themselves out. Family is where the foundation begins!*
>
> *Jerome F. White*

Have you ever asked yourself whom can one depend on? Without your family, whom can you depend on? Sometimes family is all you have. Many times due to the political bureaucracy and the financial corruption, the federal and state

13

governments are only allowed to do so much for its American constituents in regards to laws being passed. If there is peace, love and stability within our own household, the bureaucracy will have little impact causing a true uproar within our homes. The family is the cornerstone to which provides a stable foundation for our children, who are our future and will be the catalyst to making our country a better place for all people.

President Theodore Roosevelt had many accomplishments during his life time and specifically during his presidency. When President Roosevelt took office, the civil war had ended approximately 36 years earlier. President Roosevelt was a governor, an explorer, a war hero, an author of thirty-five books and the 1st American to win the Nobel Peace Prize. He was the first president to fly in an airplane, ride in an automobile and to be submerged in a submarine. Nevertheless President Theodore Roosevelt did nothing to better blacks' voting rights. Although President Roosevelt believed that all men were created equal and had a profound belief in the moral fiber of the Declaration of Independence, in regard to race relations he and his administration took the long term approach to solving civil rights. He believed in the end all things will work out between whites and blacks for the common good of mankind. It should be noted that President Roosevelt was unfavorably scrutinized by the southern states for inviting Booker T. Washington to dinner at the White House. Never again during his administration did President Roosevelt invite another black man to dine with him at the White House (De Vries, et al., 2003).

President Harry S. Truman, at one time in his life was allegedly a member of the Ku Klux Klan (KKK). On February 2, 1948 President Truman said the following profound message to Congress:

We shall not...achieve the ideals for which this nation was founded so long as any American suffers discrimination...If we wish to inspire the peoples of the world whose freedom is in jeopardy, if we wish to restore hope to those who have already lost their civil liberties,... we must correct the remaining imperfections in our practice of democracy.

It can be debated but it is believed that the above message to Congress is directly linked to the horrible tragedy of Isaac Woodard Jr. This brave black World War II veteran had recently returned from his tour and was viciously attacked while still in uniform by South Carolina police. The brutal attack left Mr. Woodard Jr. blind in both eyes. This tragic event occurred on February 12, 1946 and within approximately two years President Truman desegregated the armed forces under a single secretary of defense (Hamby, et al., 2012).

When looking deep into President Woodrow Wilson's past, one must be reminded that his father (Joseph Ruggles Wilson) was a Presbyterian minister that owned slaves prior to the ending of the Civil War and the President himself was a southerner (Berg, 1985). Prior to his presidency and early in his professional career (1902 to 1910), President Wilson was the president of Princeton University. During his tenor at Princeton, he never allowed one black person to be admitted into their institution of higher learning. This is tragic in that President Wilson knew the key to blacks moving up the social ladder was via a good education (Mulder, at al., 2012). Blacks strongly supported President Wilson in his first term because they believed the President's vision of new freedom. Blacks were extremely disappointed in the actual results of President Wilson. President Wilson segregated the federal government jobs. It was believed that President Wilson betrayed blacks and pushed race relation progress back about fifty years. William Monroe Trotter, a black activist who supported President Wilson in 1912, stated the following directly to the President: *"Only two years ago you were heralded as perhaps the second Lincoln, and black leaders who supported you are hounded as false leaders and traitors to the race. What a change segregation has wrought!"* (Berg, 346). Trotter continued by asking President Wilson if his "new freedom" for whites was nothing more than "new slavery" for black citizens. It was a harsh reality for blacks to learn they couldn't rely on the federal government to bring about the right type of change at the right time to improve America. President Wilson didn't deliver. He couldn't bridge this gap and make the tough decisions regarding these issues.

During the presidency of Franklin D. Roosevelt, America was slow to adapt to segregation changes but some very tough decisions were made in the attempt to be fair. A. Philip Randolph, who was the leader of Brotherhood of Sleeping Car Porters, met with the president along with Walter White of the National Association for the Advance of Colored People (NAACP). The federal jobs within the defense industry refused to hire blacks. In protest to these unfair hiring practices, Mr. Randolph teamed with black leadership with the intentions on assembling a mass group of people to march on Washington. On June 18, 1941 President Roosevelt and Mr. Randolph met to discuss these discriminatory practices of the defense industry. It was mentioned during the meeting that blacks were ready to march on Washington in numbers 100,000 strong to protest the lack of opportunity being given to blacks in the defense industry. President Roosevelt, who was one of a kind spirit and of great diplomacy, told Mr. Randolph he couldn't implement change quickly while a march on Washington was going on and encouraged Randolph to please end the march. Mr. Randolph mentioned to the President that new laws can be put into place through executive order and unless these discriminatory practices ended they would march. In addition, Mr. Randolph told the President that he had promised his supporters he would not accept anything less than an executive order. On June 25, 1941, President Roosevelt signed the executive order ending discrimination in the defense industry (Morgan, 1985). By the time the President's three terms in office ended, the majority of blacks that were affiliated with the Republican Party prior to Roosevelt's first term had switch to the Democratic Party.

President Franklin D. Roosevelt was in command during World War II. After the bombing of Pearl Harbor by Japan, it seemed inevitable that America would enter the war. Sadly, approximately 120,000 Japanese in California were place in internment camps due to fear of espionage. Approximately half of the Japanese that were forced to move and denied due process were American citizens (Morgan, 1985).

President Roosevelt was instrumental in establishing the New Deal programs and reforms. This opened opportunities for all less privileged Americans, including blacks. Unemployed farmers and workers in rural areas found work. During this period many blacks migrated from the south to northern states for manufacturing factory jobs (Maney, 2012). These new programs coupled with the ending of World War II itself brought America out of the great depression.

Brown versus the Board of Education was decided one year after President Dwight D. Eisenhower took office. According to Carlson (2006), "… it's best to say he was not an obstructionist, nor a hero on *Brown* and related issues." The Civil Rights Act of 1964, Medicare (Title XVIII) & Medicaid (Title XIX) implementation were put into effect during President Lyndon

B. Johnson's administration. President Johnson took a very practical approach with his great ability to compromise and negotiate to get bills passed. Below is an excerpt of a conversation which supports this fact with a discussion between at the time Vice-President Johnson and Senator John C. Stennis, who was the U.S. Senator from the state of Mississippi:

> *"Well you know, John, the other day a sad thing happened. Helen Williams and her husband, Gene, who have been working for me for many years, drove my official car from Washington down to Texas, the Cadillac limousine of the vice-president of the United States. They drove through your state, and when they got hungry, they stopped at grocery stores on the edge of town in colored areas and bought Vienna sausage and beans and ate them with a plastic spoon. And when they had to go to the bathroom, they would stop, pull off on a side road, and Helen Williams, an employee of the vice-president of the United States, would squat in the road to pee. And you know, John, that's just bad. That's just wrong. And there ought to be something to change that. And it seems to me that if people in Mississippi don't just change it voluntarily, that it's just going to be necessary to change it by law."*

The above discussion did not persuade Senator Stennis to change his mind on trying to block Civil Rights bill from passing (Miller, 1981). Old ways die hard, but the Civil Rights Act of 1964 passed despite efforts to thwart it.

John Fitzgerald Kennedy was America's 35th President. The

time had come for major civil rights change. Approximately 100 years had passed since Abraham Lincoln signed the Emancipation Proclamation yet blacks were still fighting most of the same discriminatory and racist American practices against them. Young blacks had had enough. The time for change was now! Several key people and organizations made this change occur. Martin Luther King Jr., the Student Nonviolent Coordinating Committee (SNCC), the Congress of Racial Equality (CORE), the Freedom Riders and "sit-ins" at lunch counters throughout the south efforts made it happen. President Kennedy also contributed to this change by using his authority strategically during the Freedom Riders demonstrations and "sit-ins". It was divine timing. Many of civil rights protest were broadcast on national television. President Kennedy wanted to comply with the black's demands but he also wanted to appease his southern voters that supported him. President Kennedy's hands were tied and tough decisions had to be made. President Kennedy made the tough decision. He expressed the following moral statement to Congress:

> *"In short, every American ought to have the right to be treated as he would wish to be treated, as one would wish his children to be treated." And injustice demanded action…"Those who do nothing are inviting shame as well as violence. Those who act boldly are recognizing right as well as reality".*

At the time, President Kennedy was the youngest president ever elected. In addition, he was the first President affiliated with the Catholic faith. President Kennedy gave America hope, faith and dreams for a better society. On November 22, 1963 President Kennedy was assassinated. That day, everything

President Kennedy fought for was locked into the minds of the America people forever. America's heart was broken. Within a year of his death, the Civil Rights Act of 1964 passed with the signing by President Johnson. Senator Allen J. Ellender of Louisiana said the bill would not have passed if the president had lived. In the minds of America, President Kennedy's sacrifice of his own life made this happen (Reeves, 1991). For this reason many blacks of this era considered President John F. Kennedy "their" president.

President John F. Kennedy truly tried to fix some of the wrongs associated with slavery. In 1961, he issued Executive Order 10925, which states, in part, that government contractors should "take affirmative action to ensure that applicants are employed, and employees are treated during employment, without regard to their race, creed, color, or national origin" (UCI, 2015). It seems that, for blacks, the order was never implemented the way Kennedy intended.

Blacks had been brought to America with the specific intent to be slaves; no other group in America had entered the country for that purpose. Merriam-Webster defines reparations as the practice of improving the educational and job opportunities of members of groups that have not been treated fairly in the past because of their race, sex, etc. One of the greatest injustices in the United States was slavery. There are arguments for and against reparations. According to World Book Encyclopedia (2012 ed.), reparations are efforts, usually by a nation's government, to make up for harm or wrongdoing that has occurred in the past. Reparations often include the payment of money or the return of property to individuals or groups. For example, after World War II, West Germany and United States paid reparations to a group of people. West Germany paid $800 million to Jews and the State of Israel for the gross mistreatment by the Nazis. In addition, the United

States paid $20,000 to each surviving Japanese Americans which were forced into internment camps during World War II. Accordingly, the United States harmed previous Africans for supporting slavery. Liberals and conservatives argue slavery and the aftermath of legalized segregation was ultimately wrong. Reparations were never paid for that free labor given by an entire race of people. With the amendments in 1967 by President Johnson to Executive Order 11246, which prohibited sex discrimination by federal contractors and expanded job opportunities for women, new opportunities would now expand to minority groups. Blacks were redefined as a minority by the federal government, and that designation comprised all minorities, including woman. Affirmative action has helped all minorities, but white women particularly. In a study compiled by the Centers of American Progress in the 1st quarter of 2012, the unemployment rate for white women was 7.2%, Latina women 11.4% and black women 13.3%. In addition, the United States Labor Department states white women are the primary beneficiaries from affirmative action (Daniels, 2014). Therefore, the question should be asked, if a system goes from a white Anglo Saxon protestant male system to a system where white women receive favor, has anything really changed? There are still white Americans in control. Things have definitely changed for the better for African Americans, but America still has a long way to go. Since America's "Founding Fathers" based the founding of this great nation upon biblical principles, let's take a look at what the Lord says about husbands, wives, and family.

In order to determine how America should have changed in the 21st century, we can consult the biblical principles upon which this nations was said to be founded. First Timothy 5:8 says *But if any provide not for his own, and specially for those of his house, he hath denied the faith, and is worse than an infidel.* First Corinthians 11:3 says, *But I would have you know, that the head of every man is Christ; and the head of the woman is the man; and the head of Christ is God.* Ephesians 5:25 says *Husbands, love your wives, even as Christ also loved the church, and gave himself for it.* Colossians 3:19 says *Husbands, love your wives, and be not bitter against them.* God clearly wanted man to take care of his wife and family. This duty to care for the family is deeply rooted to the bread winner of the family. With affirmative action giving the true benefits abundantly to white women and the North American Free Trade Agreement (NAFTA) taking jobs over to Mexico, Canada and China, how in America can a man who sees no benefit from either program take care of his family as God intended? NAFTA's objective was to abandon obstacles to trade and investment between the U.S., Canada and Mexico. In 1990 negotiations between these three nations began under direction of the forty first U.S. President George H. W. Bush but the actual signing of NAFTA occurred on December 8th, 1993 under U.S. President Bill Clinton. Prior to signing NAFTA, President Clinton established two additional laws which protected workers and the environment. These two additions by President Clinton were called the North American Agreement on Labor Cooperation (NAALC) and the North American Agreement on Environmental Cooperation (NAAEC), respectfully. NAFTA would remove the U.S.-Mexico tariffs within 10 years with the exception of some U.S. agricultural exports to Mexico, which would be eliminated within 15 years.

Many believed that the ratification of NAFTA would create more economic growth, equality, expansion, remove foreign trade barriers and start the beginning of more global competition. It was hoped that NAFTA would help the United States maintain its middle class while assisting the world build their middle class simultaneously. Did this "hope" actually come true? No! NAFTA caused several hundred thousand jobs to move to Mexico. In addition, with globalization being a reality, NAFTA was the catalyst for negotiations with China's lower wage worker employers (Faux, et al., 2013).

Beyond a shadow of a doubt, there are too many black males in prison. Although there are a lot of great husbands and fathers in America, American males have generally failed the American woman in fulfilling God's plan for family, and the federal government hasn't made it any easier for the plan to be fulfilled. Prisons are being constructed by the government at the cost of 700 million dollars a year. Although education is known to be the key to success in America, approximately 143,000 black men were incarcerated while 463,700 were in educational institutions of higher learning in 1980. Let's fast forward to the year 2000 where approximately 800,000 black men were incarcerated while approximately 600,000 were registered in higher learning institutions (Boothe, 2007). Let's take a look at different countries people incarceration rates per 100,000 citizens: currently America has 700 people per 100,000 citizens; France has 85 people per 100,000 citizens; Japan has 48 people per 100,000 citizens; Great Britain, which has one of the toughest penal systems in Western Europe, has approximately 140 people per 100,000 citizens. America has substantially more people in the prison system than China whose population is four times higher. Please note that China has 1.3 billion residents. The United States of America has more blacks imprisoned than the entire black population of the country of Canada (Boothe, 2007). Below is an excerpt from the book written by Demico Boothe called "Why Are So Many Black Men in Prison?":

> *A black boy born today has about a 1 in 1,250*
> *chance of being a NFL football player; a 1 in*

*4,600 chance of becoming a NBA player; a 1 in
2,000 chance of getting a Ph.D. in engineering,
mathematics, or the physical sciences; a 1 in 548
chance of becoming a doctor; a 1 in 195 chance
of becoming a lawyer; and a 1 in 53 chance of
becoming a teacher. That same black boy has a
1 in 13 chance of going to prison before he turns
20; a 1 in 6 chance of going to prison at least
once before he dies; a 1 in 3 chance of becoming
an ex-felon; a 1 in 7 chance of never graduating
from high school; a 5 in 6 chance of never
graduating from college; and a 1 in 2 chance of
becoming a drug abuser.*

We, as Americans, still have a lot of work to do. In short, black men can't love their wives and children as well as take care of their families if they're in prison.

Ancestors play a major role in the behavior of their descendants. At the most basic level, none of us would exist today without the sacrifices and survival of our ancestors. Have you ever wondered what it would be like to talk to your ancestors or to ask them how it felt to experience a certain event? If you had a chance to talk to your oldest known ancestor, what would you say? My four grandparents—Erma, Willie, Senie, and Jesse—paid the price for their descendants, and, before my grandparents were born, their ancestors paid a price for them. To look back and see how our ancestors persevered from day to day survival through hard core sacrifices and experiences is laudable. It is the trickling down effect. Merriam-Webster defines the trickling down effect as relating to or being an effect caused gradually by remote or indirect influences. All the ordeals our ancestors endured were real; their experiences affect generation after generation after generation. Their past experiences influence our current behavior.

Jesse White's great grandfather, Nathaniel White, died on May 18th, 1884. Jesse White never knew his great grandfather. Below is a letter written by Jesse White's grandson to Nathaniel White in an attempt to talk to his passed on ancestor:

February 2016

Dear great, great, great grandfather Nathaniel White,

What a blessing it is today to write you this letter. I hope all is going well with you and you are in good spirits. This letter is in celebration of your 200th birthday. We as people truly need to honor that. Happy birthday great, great, great grandfather Nathaniel. Without you and your wife Charlotte surviving and enduring all that you encountered, we would not be here today. I wanted to take a moment of your time to thank you for your sacrifices. It is with great respect when I say this. You worked most of your life as a slave on the Frierson plantation and during the time of your servitude were not paid for those laborious services. It is unimaginable. Slavery was a system based on greed and unfair treatment to Africans in America.

I have a million questions to ask you great, great, great grandfather Nathaniel. Not sure where to even start with all my inquiries. God and the Holy Spirit can only guide me in writing to you. I have asked God to help me. I observed in some correspondences with your name on it, you went by the name of Nat, which is short for Nathaniel. I have to admit when I first heard that you're also known as Nat, I thought about Nat Turner. When you first received the news Nat Turner had a successful slave revolt in an attempt to abolish the system of slavery, what went through your mind? The actual rebellion began on August 21, 1831 but Nat Turner wasn't captured by the white militia for nearly two months later. At the time of Nat Turners rebellion, you were only 15 years old. During this time, did you notice the Frierson's not allowing you to read the Bible anymore? Or taking away your reading privileges? I am curious. What were your concerns when you first heard that Abraham Lincoln had signed the Emancipation Proclamation and Congress had passed the 13th, 14th and 15th amendments to the United States Constitution? I can only imagine the rejuvenation you must have felt. Did you anticipate the southern states rebellion which actually occurred after the ratification of all these profound laws?

Excitedly, I am very proud to say that I have kept your traditions alive. Particularly the tradition I have fulfilled is one wife, one job. My love for my wife of sixteen years is as great as the love you had for your wife, great, great, great grandmother Charlotte. My wife and I have two children who are included in your over five hundred descendants. Believe me when I say great, great, great grandfather Nathaniel you set a precedent in our family and we truly want to continue the great traditions you established.

Another question, great, great, great grandfather Nathaniel, during the winter time, have you ever noticed how snow builds up on the tree branches; how cold rain turned to ice on tree branches; how the build up from snow and ice bends the branches of trees; and how over time the branches snap with an extremely loud sound? Did that scare you as much as it scared me? Have you ever looked into the sky late at night and noticed the brightest light you have was the light from the moon? Isn't that awesome? Have you ever looked in the sky late at night and noticed those three stars lined up by each other? The Egyptians observed those same stars line up five thousand years ago. The three pyramids of Giza are proclaimed to be positioned perfectly to that the 3 stars of Orion. The other day I noticed those three stars. How profound is that these stars were viewed by you, the Egyptians and I?

Tell me about some of the primary meals you have cooked for yourself? Have you ever taken the ashes from the wood of your wood burning stove or chimney and cooked sweet potatoes separately? From what I hear, the process takes time. You sort of get the chance to perform two task at once. Did you place your wood ashes on a separate iron utensil and place the sweet potato on top and occasionally rotate your sweet potato in order to evenly cook it? Did you have to regularly take those ashes replace them with hotter ashes

Page 1 of 3

Figure 1. A Descendant's Letter to His Ancestor

while simultaneously rotating your sweet potato? I will tell you one thing great, great, great grandfather Nathaniel and I am sure you would agree, the sweet potato is some good eating if you cook it right. Although tripe, hog mog (maw), chittlins and hot water corn bread are not the healthiest meals available, I love to eat it. I bet you could share several tips on how to survive outdoors.

Recently I have researched quite a few documents in an attempt to find the names of your parents. I have not had luck. What is your mother's name? What was your father's name? I would have been delighted to have known their names. When the Frierson's took ownership of you, what made you keep your last name "White" and not take on the "Frierson" last name? I have plenty of theories but I would like to hear it directly from you. As it has been said, were you "sold down the river" after a slave auction? Below is a map of your migration from South Carolina to Lowndes County, Alabama and then later from Alabama to Frierson, Louisiana:

Please tell me about that experience. Were both trips done during the summer time? How long did both trips take? Combined miles related to your great migration was over 900 miles. Based on the records I viewed you made the trip to Lowndes County Alabama from South Carolina when you were not a father. You had your first child around 1845 in Lowndes County, Alabama. Your first child was a son whom you named Jesse, which is whom my grandfather is named after. Why did you name your son Jesse? Is it possible your father name was Jesse? I was proud to learn you were born in South Carolina. How appalled were you to be counted as three fifths a person for representation purposes? Politically speaking, were you a Republican? My first guess is the answer to that question is a "yes". There is nothing wrong with following Abraham Lincoln's political party. I have visited the DeSoto Parish Court House for voting records during the period affiliated when voting rights were granted to you. Unless one is a "Very Important Person" or VIP, voting records this far back are not saved. Therefore, I found no records of voting in DeSoto Parish at any time pertaining to you. Sorry for that sad news. I would love to know if you were able to vote without major conflict. The 15th amendment gave you as well as myself that right.

What did you do for fun? Did you enjoy hunting or fishing? Could you play any musical instruments? Did you enjoy reading or listening to poetry? I love poetry. I would like for you to share your thoughts with me regarding a beautiful poem that was eventually put to lovely music. For now, I will only share with you one of the verses of the poem, which has three verses:

> *Lift every voice and sing*
> *Till earth and heaven ring,*
> *Ring with the harmonies of Liberty;*

MY FOUR GRANDPARENTS

February 2016

Let our rejoicing rise,
High as the listening skies,
Let it resound loud as the rolling sea.
Sing a song full of the faith that the dark past has taught us,
Sing a song full of the hope that the present has brought us,
Facing the rising sun of our new day begun,
Let us march on till victory is won.

Isn't the above poem beautiful? It was written by James Weldon Johnson in 1899 and put to music later by his brother John Rosamond Johnson. What a true masterpiece it is. The entire song was later claimed to be the national anthem for African Americans due to its cry for liberation.

Currently during this millennium, race is becoming less of a factor in marriage. Couples in 2016 will marry anyone they love regardless of race. Based on the history books I read, this was not the case in the 19th and 20th century. I've learned white men hated black men dating their white woman during your era? How true is this? Have you ever heard of black men and white women that broke the courting rules? I have been told from oral traditions that the white man would regularly rape black woman. How true is this? Is there any chance that some of the black women consented to be a lover of her white man? Could some of those experience been true love or even consensual lust? One thing that is true is white mobs would lynch black men for sleeping with white woman, consenting or not. There are pictures to prove this fact of lynching in history books all over. Have you every witness or known a black man that was lynched? Sometimes, I am not sure what to believe in regards to race relations during the 19th century. The human spirit never changes and Gods love always prevailed.

Lastly, great, great, great grandfather Nathaniel because of your sacrifices, I will never take for granted my freedom, a place to lay my head, the right to vote, my citizenship as an American, fair pay for a living wage, the importance and need for cohesiveness and love for family, the United States as a nation of laws and every meal I eat. By the way, on a side note, we have a black president. God whispered to me the other day that He answered your prayer when He ordained the "swearing in" ceremony of Barack Hussain Obama. Thanks for all your prayers great, great, great grandfather Nathaniel. I know you prayed for me, your descendants and I know God was listening. Our God is a patient God. He doesn't perform events when we ask Him to but He is always right on time. Please write me soon great, great, great grandfather Nathaniel but if not by letter, spiritually is fine also. Take care of yourself and again thank you for everything.

Sincerely,

Your great, great, great grandson

The 13th Amendment was ratified in 1865. It declared that 'neither slavery nor involuntary servitude, except as a punishment for crime whereof the party shall have been duly convicted, shall exist within the United States, or any place subject to their jurisdiction' (US Library of Congress, 2015). Well over a century after the abolition of slavery, voting rights for blacks in DeSoto Parish were still being dishonored at the polls. As late in the 20th century as the early 1950s, in DeSoto Parish during the voting process, whites asked black voters to recite portions of the Declaration of Independence or the Bill of Rights. If would-be voters did not pass this pre-voter registration test, they were not allowed to vote. Some blacks who did pass the memory test were still not allowed to register or vote. This blatant injustice was an example of America's democracy not working at all.

Reverend Horace L. Dickerson, the pastor of Bethel Baptist Church in Frierson, Louisiana, was a brave, proud, and upstanding person who wanted change. In 1952, he was beaten and left for dead on a roadside near Gloster, Louisiana by a white mob because he assisted black citizens with voter registration in DeSoto Parish. Although Reverend Dickerson was left for dead, he actually survived to tell his story. Reverend Dickerson was a contractor who had built many churches, which included but were not limited to the modern church buildings of Bethel Baptist Church, Antioch Baptist Church, and Good Hope Presbyterian Church in DeSoto Parish. In addition, Reverend Dickerson built the homes of Jesse White and Edith Chiphe, which currently stand on White Springs Road in Frierson. Reverend Dickerson would sometimes show the scars from the tragic event when he was beaten by the white mob to emphasize how far voting rights had progressed from that time. Reverend Dickerson died in July 1994 and is buried at New Bethlehem Baptist Church in Gloster, Louisiana.

The journey for African Americans in northern Louisiana has not been easy. Once African Americans were allowed to become police officers within the force, they could only arrest African Americans and not white criminals. Some history is hard to believe but this is the way life was over one hundred years after the ratification of the 13th Amendment.

DeSoto Parish has come a long way. My four grandparents' lives exemplify the progress made by African Americans in these parishes.

One of the greatest gifts is growing up knowing your grandparents. We are born to four genetic grandparents, eight genetic great-grandparents, sixteen genetic great-great-grand-parents, thirty-two genetic great-great-great grandparents and sixty-four genetic great-great-great-great-grandparents. Rudy Giuliani once said, "What children need most are the essentials that grandparents provide in abundance. They give unconditional love, kindness, patience, humor, comfort and lessons in life."

In the African American family, grandparents are essential to giving balance within the family. Often times, grandparents, or the grandmother and/or grandfather live with their children, as they age and are no longer able to live independently. In those cases, the grandparents are the story tellers of family history. The grandfather may teach the grandson how to fix things or work outdoors. The grandmother sits patiently and shares family recipes that have been passed down or demonstrates the importance of perseverance, kindness and meekness. It's those moments that linger. It's those moments that transform. It's those moments you never forget. They sometime share the long stories that begin with, "when I was your age..." Sometimes it's hard to imagine they were ever your age. Many times the parents do not recognize these people called grandparents. "You never allowed us to do that" are exclaimed with indignation! Because grandparents can smile and say, "They're not my children", they say as they slip us a cookie before dinner.

Fortunately, grandparents can sit back and enjoy watching the grandkids grow up. They've experience parenthood and often never would desire to repeat raising a child in puberty.

They become the trusted source of information. They listen objectively with a loving heart. Patience and caring is their mantle. They mostly recognize their children or themselves in their grandchildren. Grandparents are the mirror of their children and see the reflection of themselves in their grandchildren. Grandchildren are just overjoyed to have someone else to love them unconditionally. Fortunate are those who have known all four of their grandparents.

Grandparents have a way of not doing anything wrong, of giving grandchildren the utmost love and attention. Grandparents are simply unforgettable. In order to give more focus on their individuality, my four grandparents have been discussed separately. Since all four grandparents struggled and persevered through life experience up through their deaths, it was not always easy separating them because both couples did their best to be a team. Knowing all that they endured, it makes their love even more amazing and special. Their lives and experiences have been explained in the following order: 1st Erma Freemen (paternal grandmother), 2nd Bud Green (maternal grandfather), 3rd Senie Winters (maternal grandmother) and 4th Jesse White (paternal grandfather). Now it is time for you to read and share their journey. Therefore, let's begin with Erma Freeman, the youngest of the four grandparents.

Erma Freeman:
The sweetest woman

Erma Freeman White was born on March 25, 1918 in Grand Cane, Louisiana. She was the third of the eight children of James Freeman and Mackie Murray. Erma's siblings were Minnie, Edward, Ashton, Curtis, Mary, Eunice, and Maxie. Mackie, Erma's mother, died in March of 1927 while giving birth to her son Maxie. Mackie was estimated to be twenty-nine years old when she died. Erma was approximately nine when her mother died.

In the 1920 census, when only four of his eight children with Mackie had been born, Erma's father James listed himself and his children as mulatto. Mackie Murray listed herself in the census as black. It appears as though there was some uncertainty about how James should classify the race of his children. Within the 1920 census, James and Mackie Freeman listed their children with the letter B, which stands for black. In addition, the letter M, which stands for mulatto, is next to the letter B. As an adult, Erma made it clear her mother Mackie was a dark-complexioned black woman.

Mackie's parents were named Henry Murray and Della Preston. It is said that Papa Henry Murray could have been from east Texas, but that fact has not been verified. In addition, some versions of the family's history contend that Henry was from a town called Dodie Hill, Louisiana, which is near a town called Monday, Louisiana. Both towns are so small that they are not listed in current maps. Henry and Della had twelve children, including Mackie: Ulysses, Hester, Mittie, Owen, Mercie D., Mattie, Tom, Marville, Otto, Della, and Texas. Two uncounted children of Henry and Della were taken home to be with the Lord as children. Eight of their twelve children were listed in the 1900 US census. Although there are not many records of Henry's and Della's parents, it is known that Henry's parents were born in Louisiana. There is a little more information on Della's parents. Her father, who was named Baker Preston, was born around 1820. Baker was from Georgia. Della's mother's name was Sallie Preston. She was born around 1835 and was also from the state of Georgia. Both of Sallie's parents were from Georgia. Both of Baker's parents were from North Carolina.

It is unknown the exact date of the passing of Della Preston, but Papa Henry Murray married Beatrice Salone. They would have four children named Madilee, Juanita, David, and Maurice. Papa Henry Murray had five other children whose names were Henry Jr., Mary, Willie, Lucy, and Ophelia. Therefore, Papa Henry Murray had at least 21 children by at least three women, two of whom were his wives. Papa Henry Murray is said to have died on August 22, 1925 at around the age of 64. Papa Henry Murray is buried at Mount Zion Baptist Church in Kingston, LA.

Erma's father, James Freeman, was born on June 4, 1893 to Will Freeman and Mary Ware-Freeman. James joined Bond Chest Methodist Church in 1909. Later, he joined Mount Zion Baptist Church. After Mackie's death, Erma's father James Freeman married Tillah White-Freeman. Together, they had four children, whose names were Kiah, Carrie, Carolyn, and Willie James. In total, therefore, James had 12 children. Taking on a new stepmother is never easy, but Tillah White-Freeman was said to be a very loving mother to Mackie's children; she loved them as her own. James was a great husband and provider to his children. He provided for his family via farming of crops. His faith was strong and it carried him throughout his life. James never wavered on that which was unseen or the assurance of things hoped for. James became a member of Summer Hill Baptist Church in 1941, where he served as a deacon until his death. James Freeman served as superintendent of the Sunday school department for 21 years. In addition, James served as chairman of the Deacons' Board for 34 years. He would spend his later years in Pelican, Louisiana where it was rumored that his land had so much oil on it, that oil saturated people's shoes while they walked on his property. James Freeman died in December of 1976 at the age of 83. James Freeman lived by the biblical verse of Psalm 23, verse 4, which says: "Yea, though I walk through the valley of the Shadow of Death, I will fear no evil; for thou art with me. Thy rod and thy staff they comfort me."

Erma accepted Christ in her life and was baptized at an early age at Mount Zion Baptist Church, under the leadership of Reverend J.P. Powell. She was a descendant of some of the original members. Mount Zion, which has great history, was organized January 19, 1870 in the home of Brother Wesley Hall. Based on Erma's childhood church records, the church was named Mount Zion Baptist Church during the first conference on June 6, 1870 under a brush arbor near the old Lacy Quarters. Reverend Stephen Presley was elected as the first pastor. During a conference held on September 24, 1870 Brother Ben Ware and Brother Bob Roberts were elected as deacons. Brother Henry Samuel was the first clerk. From a motion Sister Abbey Ware was elected Mother of the church during conference on July 22, 1871. The church motto, which was selected by Pastor John H. Nash is "Standing on His Promises" 1st John 2:25.

The church body purchased additional property with clear deeds and titles, six acres more or less, for the expansion of programs to meet the needs of the people. The church building has changed over time. Mount Zion members worshipped in a family home, a brush arbor, a log cabin (a door was placed in the side of the cabin), a box house, first frame building, second frame building and the present brick building. The brick building was rebuilt in 1966 during the leadership of the late Reverend Louis Sweeney and built by a church member, the late Deacon E.J. Ware, Jr.

The Northwest Baptist Association held its first session at Mount Zion during the leadership of the late Reverend. I.S. Imbers. Reverend B.M. Morris, eighth pastor, served as vice-president of the Northwest Baptist Association.

Pastors and duration of service: Stephen Presley was the first pastor and was called the second time as the fifth pastor serving seven years; Jefferson Gilmer was elected pastor on January 26, 1873 and served until death (time not given); James Christian, two months; W.M. Preston, (time not given for first term); W.M. Preston, four years and four months his second term; R.H. Walker, three years; Nathan Oliver, four years; E.W. Simpson (time not given); S.S. Fuller, until death (time not given); March Williams, five years; B.H. Taylor, twelve years; J.P. Powell, nine years; H.S. James, one year; D.V. Martin, two months; Hines Wilson, four year and eight months; I.S. Imbers, two years one month; Kermit R. Reed, five years and four months; Ludd Flanigan, four years and nine months; L.D. Sudds eight years and two months; Louis Sweeney, 19 years; Cleveland Douglas, eleven years; and John H. Nash, Sr. D.TH. from March 1996 until present.

With roots so deeply tied to the church it is apparent why Erma's faith was so strong. As a child, Erma attended Grand Cane Elementary School, but she never attended high school. Survival was most important to her family, which explains why she finished school up through the eighth grade.

James Freeman and his family would attend family

functions of Hezekiah White Sr. when Erma was a young lady. These gatherings led to the introduction of Jesse White and Erma Freeman. Her future husband, Jesse, fell in love with Erma at first sight. She was beautiful, demure, shapely, soft-spoken, honest, loving, God fearing, came from a well-respected family, and had gorgeous hazel eyes. Because Erma worked her parents' farm when she was a child, she was very knowledgeable of the farming industry. With all of these attributes and having a strong work ethic, too, what man wouldn't desire this kind of woman? Jesse pursued her heavily, Erma fell in love with him, and the rest was history. Figure 2 is a copy of the marriage license solidifying the union between Erma and Jesse.

MARRIAGE LICENSE No. 12259

STATE OF LOUISIANA, PARISH OF DE SOTO

To any Minister of the Gospel, Judge or Justice of the Peace, who is authorized to celebrate Marriage in the Parish of DeSoto

GREETING:

You are hereby authorized to celebrate Marriage between

JESSIE WHITE *and* ERMA FREEMAN

to join them together in lawful wedlock,

Given under my hand and seal of office, on the 7th day of November 19 36.

O. A. Flanders
Dy. Clerk of District Court

STATE OF LOUISIANA, PARISH OF DESOTO
PROCESS VERBAL OF MARRIAGE

BE IT Remembered, that by virtue of a License issued by the Clerk of the District Court for DeSoto Parish, Louisiana, I have celebrated marriage between

Mr. Jessie White *and* M Erma Freeman

and have joined them together in Holy Wedlock, according to law, the _____ day

of _____ A. D., 1936

WITNESSES	PARTIES
Hermon Hudson	Jessie White
H. K. White Jr.	Erma Freeman
RenaC. Marshall Ware	Minister of the Gospel or Justice of the Peace.

STATE OF LOUISIANA, PARISH OF DESOTO
MARRIAGE CERTIFICATE

I HEREBY CERTIFY, That I have celebrated marriage in accordance with the laws of Louisiana, between

Mr. Jessie White _and_ M Erma Freeman

and have joined them together in Holy Matrimony. Thus given under my hand in the Parish of DeSoto, State of

Louisiana, on this the 5 day of November 19 _____

Minister of the Gospel or Justice of the Peace.

Figure 2. Marriage license of Erma Freeman and Jesse White

Erma and Jesse married on November 8, 1936 at Mount Zion Baptist Church in Kingston, LA. Together, they had twelve children, including a set of twins: Jeremiah, Mackie, Hezekiah III, John, James, Lossie, Curley V., Jessie, Mercie, Bertha, Ralph, and Clara. Their first child was born October 26, 1937 and the last child was born June 7, 1951.

Twelve children in under fourteen years was a tremendous challenge for the couple. Erma was a homemaker throughout her marriage. In addition to being a homemaker, Erma would farm on her land to assist Jesse with the production of crops. Erma never knew how to drive a car, although during her lifespan, women her age knew how to drive. Erma chose to live her life in a passive way and her husband Jesse wanted to be in control. Raising a family is not always easy, and the complexities of marriage existed between Jesse and Erma. Deep inside, every parent wants his or her children to have more than they had in the previous generation. This desire is what motivated Erma. She sacrificed for the family. She sacrificed for her children. One of Erma's favorite old sayings was: "*A woman gotta do what a woman gotta do.*"

The following poem symbolizes the core of Erma:

Raising a family can be hard
We will make it because I rely on the Lord
If you are selfish it may be best to never marry
There are burdens but they're place on God to carry
Am I doing the right thing, I didn't always know
But now looking back, I did reap what I sow
Now I am thankful because I did not listen to what they say
My faith paid off, I wouldn't have it any other way

Church Service

Jesse and Erma's family was known as a privileged family although everything they earned came from hard work. The family was an active member of Good Hope Presbyterian Church in Frierson, Louisiana. Sunday was a very busy day. It began with Sunday school and morning worship. It was mandatory that the children attend church. A typical Sunday church service was not long and was over prior to two o'clock in the afternoon. Church services were family oriented. For example, the pastor or superintendent would announce the sick, create a prayer list, pray for the sick and shut-in, sing songs, discuss various announcements, following the Presbyterian protocol. On Sunday evenings, the entire family would go back to church if there was a special program or some type of women's or men's function. Everyone was dressed in their Sunday best throughout the year. After church, everyone would prepare for dinner. The children couldn't wait to dig into the Sunday dinner meal. Every Wednesday evening there was Bible study and choir rehearsal. Erma's children sung in the choir.

Each year, one of the bigger events was the Vacation Bible School. This is where Good Hope invited the youth in the community to participate in learning the stories from the Bible. Another big yearly event was revival week; church services were from Monday through Friday evening. Revival week was an event where one would renew their relationship with God. Several churches of various denominations throughout DeSoto Parish would attend. Revival week entailed singing and praying, ending in a sermon from the preacher. Church members would serve food from the backs of their cars or trucks to feed the congregation. Another important event was the baptizing of new members. There was a Presbyterian protocol which members had to complete prior to baptism. A catechism was provided to children to assist them in better understanding the Bible.

Each year on Easter Sunday, church members participated in an early sunrise service. This was a purposeful event which encouraged members or Christians to walk as intimately as possible through the experience of Jesus Christ. Its focus was to celebrate Jesus's resurrection. All members would show up to church around five in the morning. For Christmas morning service, church members would also celebrate the birth of Christ at Good Hope. The principle reason of going to church on Christmas morning was to give thanks first and to remove the commercialization from this sacred event. This same format is applicable even in the twenty first century.

Education

Erma and Jesse developed a true foundation, all centered on their family. This foundation was based on giving the children a stable home based on love, good moral values, and godly principles. Consistency was the key component of their well-run family. On a typical weekday, Erma woke up at sunrise to get the children ready and out the door for school. The gender roles were well defined. Erma's husband Jesse and five sons would feed the animals on their farm each morning. In addition, they performed all the carpentry work and outdoor repairs. The seven girls were responsible for indoor activities such as cooking, washing clothes, sewing clothes, and cleaning the home. All of Erma and Jesse's children graduated from Second Ward High School in Gloster, LA. Second Ward School started in the kindergarten and went all the way through twelfth grade. Their oldest son spent two years at DeSoto Parish High School (originally called DeSoto Parish Training School) in Mansfield but graduated from high school at Second Ward which opened at the beginning of his senior year. Prior to Second Ward's opening, he caught the school bus to Mansfield, LA which was approximately 17 miles one way. Some of Erma and Jesse's older children attended Gravel Point Elementary and Frierson Junior High School before Second Ward was built.

During the day, Erma would work the family farm on their land. She performed household duties quickly and efficiently and prepared supper well before sunset. The older children would perform chores and were responsible for delegating duties to their younger siblings. Everyone had a chore no matter their age. This was the family's synergy: the work–chore interaction among all the individual children combined was greater than the sum of their individual efforts.

Once they were old enough, the children would come home from school and work the farm. Farming on the family land included but was not limited to raising a variety of crops and cotton picking. All the children had some involvement in the cotton picking operation. If a child was around four years old, he or she would sit on the cotton sack and just be dragged around on it as the older children picked the cotton and placed it in the sack. Children five and older had their own cotton sacks and were expected to try and fill with cotton. The children were busy with picking cotton until close to sunset or time for supper. After supper, children would complete their homework and other responsibilities.

That was Erma's routine. It was all about everyone working and being responsible. This work ethic was centered on a basic principle expressed in Benjamin Franklin's common-sense rhyme: "Early to bed, and early to rise makes a [person] healthy, wealthy, and wise."

It must be noted that Erma's husband, Jesse, would seasonally and regularly be the first in the Frierson community to gin a bail of cotton. Being first in the community to gin a bail of cotton was a status symbol. It implied that your farm was efficient, timely and productive. To gin a bail of cotton was basically the farmer processing their cotton via the cotton gin by separating the seeds from the cotton. In some cases, the seeds from the cotton could be used for next year's harvest and the cotton would be used to sale. Jesse would sell his own cotton for his own farming profits. Ecclesiastes 3:2 says: a *time to plant and a time to uproot*. Timing was everything.

Education was important to Erma. She insisted that all 12 of her children finish high school and attend college. The two who did not go college after leaving the nest were still required to take up a trade or a unique skill that would give them careers to allow them to provide for themselves.

Independence, along with interdependence, was important to Erma, who grew up at a time when it was typical for blacks to be teachers or preachers. Both were prestigious occupations but this limitation in career opportunities was primarily due to segregation, discrimination, and racism. Erma and Jesse lived well within this segregated system. Their desire for their oldest son was that he would someday become a preacher, a vocation he never chose to pursue.

Because DeSoto Parish is located in northern Louisiana and schools were segregated during the time that Erma and Jesse were rearing their children, Erma was adamant about her children being educated and having the opportunity to better themselves. Grambling College, which was only an hour drive from Frierson, was the family's choice for higher education. Several of Erma's sisters-in-law were graduates of Grambling College. The best and brightest from all over the world were attending Grambling College, and it was a great educational institution located in the south. (In 1974, the school's name changed to Grambling State University, home of world famous football coach Eddie Robinson.) Perhaps an added motivation for choosing Grambling was Ralph Waldo Emerson Jones, affectionately known as "Prez," who was Grambling's second president. He was known to have mercy on students of limited financial means.

Although Erma finished school through eighth grade, she was determined to make sure her children had opportunities that were not available to her. Erma was well aware of the limited opportunities available to women and blacks in America during this time, but she still believed firmly that education brought freedom and was the key to success in America. For Erma, it was mandatory to better oneself through education. Eight of Erma and Jesse's 12 children attended Grambling College. Six of the eight who attended Grambling College graduated with bachelor's degrees. One of Erma's daughters earned a nursing degree from Dillard University in New Orleans. All of Erma's children either mastered a trade or went to college.

Home Life

During the Christmas holidays, the entire house was festive. The house was decorated with ornaments, and gifts were placed under the Christmas tree. Every child would have his or her individual personalized stocking to hang up by Christmas Eve. If the younger children needed help with hanging their stockings, one of the older children would assist them. On Christmas Day, the children's stocking were filled with nuts, fruits, candy, boxes of raisins, and other items. Other gifts that might be included in their stocking would be a doll or truck. Rarely would anyone receive more than one gift, but the family knew they were blessed to receive that gift.

As part of the family tradition, every meal served was blessed first prior to eating. In more cases than not, Jesse would lead the prayer. An example of the blessing of the food was: "Dear Father, thank you for this food we are about to receive for the nourishment of our bodies, in Jesus's name we pray, Amen!" From there, sometimes each individual would say a Bible verse but not always. Then it was time to eat.

Erma made her own preserves. Some of the preserves she made were peach, apple, berry, mayhaw—a fruit common to wetland areas, and other fruits. These preserves were placed in glass jars and canned, which gave them an extremely long shelf life. Erma also made many of the clothes that she and her daughters wore. Her skills with a sewing machine were second to none, and with her prolific abilities, she even made her own patterns. The sewing machine she used to perform these tasks was a foot pedal model. In addition, she meticulously produced handmade quilts. She taught her daughters the quilt-making skill, too. They sewed quilts together when they finished with other work or chores. Erma exemplified the true meaning of home economics.

Erma was the true chief executive officer (CEO) of her family and she ran her home exceptionally well. She rarely had a baby sitter. One might wonder how this could be with 12 children. Erma used wisdom. When she needed to focus on a specific task at hand and the children were on her nerves, she would tell them, "go eat those berries from the mulberry tree." The mulberry tree was on her property and just far away enough that she could keep an eye on the children and still get work done. They would play, dance, and eat mulberries around the mulberry tree. Grass rarely grew around the mulberry tree because the children would circle around it regularly while eating mulberries. The children ate so many mulberries that their lips turned purple.

As Erma's children became more responsible, the older children would assist with the baby sitting. On one occasion, while the older children were babysitting and Erma was away from home, a crazy black man came onto Jesse and Erma's property. He threatened to kill all the children. He even had the audacity to walk into their home without permission and grab Jesse's rifle off the wall, where it was kept for the protection of the family. After the crazy man went on his rampage for several minutes, he put the rifle back on the wall and walked away. He never harmed the children and no one ever saw him again. After that incident, Jesse and Erma loaded all the children into Jesse's truck and took them everywhere they went, no matter the length of the task at hand. Thank God none of the children were hurt.

During church events, the most sought-after desserts

were Erma's renowned tea cakes. If any of her tea cakes came out of the oven darker than Erma liked or had the appearance of being slightly overcooked, they would not be placed in the batch that was to be brought to the church. Those tea cakes would be set aside, and could be eaten by family members and neighbors prior to attending the church event. Erma's children and neighbors were always hoping for browner than normal tea cakes, because that meant more tea cakes for them to eat. Erma made sure all the tea cakes looked great and, more importantly, tasted great. Here is the recipe for Erma's world famous tea cakes:

2 sticks of margarine
1 ½ cups of sugar
2 eggs
3 cups of flour
½ teaspoon of baking soda
1 teaspoon of baking powder
1 tablespoon of vanilla flavor
Mix all ingredients together
Grease the pan with butter
Spoon drop mixture in quarter sizes
Do not add water or milk
Pre-heat stove to 350 degrees
Cook until golden brown. Watch tea cakes continuously

Originally Erma had a wood stove, but later in life she had a butane gas stove. Therefore, tea cake cooking times can vary in the 21st century compared to the 20th century due to changes in stoves.

Erma's household was filled with plenty of food because everything the family needed was in their own fields. If they wanted cream of corn, they went out into their fields, picked their kernels of corn and brought them inside for cooking. If someone wanted okra, collard, mustard, or turnip greens, he or she went out into the field, picked the okra or green leaves and brought them home for cooking. Erma and Jesse were self-sufficient, and they capitalized on personal crops by owning their own land. God truly blessed them because they were not dependent on the deep south sharecropping system. Merriam-Webster defines sharecropper as a tenant farmer especially in the southern United States who is provided with credit for seed, tools, living quarters, and food, who works the land, and who receives an agreed share of the value of the crop minus charges. Having one's own land was beneficial, particularly if one took advantage of it. This self-sufficiency, dedication, and skill were passed down to all of Erma and Jesse's children. Hard work and actions spoke louder than words.

Boys Will Be Boys

It was very evident that Erma did not rear her girls in the exact way she reared her boys. Her sons had much more flexibility than her daughters. Have you heard the old saying about what boys are made of? "Snips and snails, and puppy dogs tails, that's what little boys are made of," or so the saying goes. According to that same verse, girls are made of "Sugar and spice and all things nice." Erma had seven daughters. They were all beautiful and fine as can be. She and Jesse were determined to protect them and do their best to keep them from the young male wolves out there. The five boys were taught to hunt, cut wood, and fish, and they learned carpentry and how to be responsible for the outdoor upkeep of the home. They were allowed more freedom with dating and risk-taking and were allowed to stay out later than their sisters.

Erma and Jesse were well aware that the young men out there wanted to court their daughters and they wanted to control their "innocence" as long as they could. Erma, the matriarch, did a great job.

Below is another poem that reflects Erma's personality:

So kind and gentle as a dove
One hundred percent made of love
Voice as calm as the sea
Her demeanor so gentle and free
Secure as can be and as soft as baby cheeks
Your forever living spirit and soul still speaks

Losing the Love of Her Life

Erma took her wedding vows seriously. When she vowed during her wedding to stay with her husband until death separated them, she meant it. Erma lost her husband in 1975. His death truly devastated her. She would live the majority of her years in the home in Frierson on White Springs Road after his death. This land was purchased solely by Jesse and Erma on November 3rd, 1969. Photo 1 is a current picture of their family home:

Photo 1. Erma and Jesse's home

On June 5th, 1970 Jesse and Erma moved off their property where they raised their children to the three bed room home above. They built themselves a home free and clear of any inherited property. Jesse's sister, Edith Chiphe, had a similar home built next door to the picture above.

What's in a Name?

Erma required her grandchildren to call her "Big Mama." No other name was acceptable. Out of respect, the grandchildren honored that. There is no greater love and protection than that of a grandmother. Later in her life, Big Mama would tell her grandchildren that she could see where all her hard work paid off. All her sacrifices and faith in God were direct results of critical decisions and actions taken by her husband and her. She was so happy about how her children turned out. The family name was honorable within the community because of her sacrifices.

Genesis

In respect to our mothers and our ties to the motherland, it can be difficult tracing our roots based on oral tradition. So much of our history has been erased. Nevertheless, the curiosity of our beginning is still there. Curiosity is definitely killing the cat. None of Erma's children ever saw their biological grandmother (Erma's mother), Mackie Murray Freeman, and Papa James Freeman did not share a lot of heritage details through oral or written communication, but the family wanted to know what the DNA results tied to Erma would reveal. In addition, Papa James Freeman had identified himself in the census as mulatto. Therefore, the family also wanted to know more about our non-African DNA roots. Are we partially white? Do we have any Native American ancestry in our genes?

These inquiries have been answered. With the assistance of Erma's oldest daughter and second-born child, Mackie Lee White Carter, we were able to find out more about Erma Freeman White's DNA origins. These results are predicated on the specific genes passed down from mother to daughter. For example, Sallie Preston passed down this specific gene called Mitochondrial DNA (mtDNA) to her daughter Della Preston, who was born around the year 1862 in DeSoto Parish, Louisiana. Della passed that gene down to her daughter Mackie Murray, who was born around the year 1897, and who passed that specific gene down to her daughter Erma Freeman White. Erma passed that specific gene down to her daughter Mackie Lee White Carter, and so on. Mackie's DNA demonstrated 86.4% Sub-Saharan African, which includes 79.2% West African. In addition, Mackie's DNA shows 13.1% European, which includes 3.9% British & Irish and 5.1% Northwestern European. There was less than 1% Native

American (0.1%) within Erma's maternal genetic makeup. In addition, there was 0.1% Southeast Asian in the maternal bloodline. Figure 3 is a graph that summarizes the DNA genetic details for Erma's maternal line:

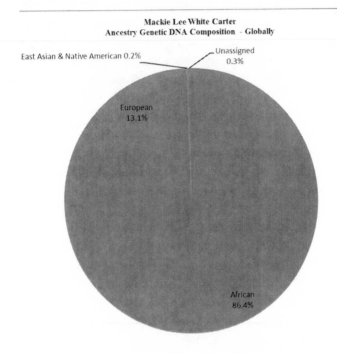

Mackie Lee White Carter
Ancestry Genetic DNA Composition - Globally

East Asian & Native American 0.2%
Unassigned 0.3%
European 13.1%
African 86.4%

Figure 3. Mackie Lee White Carter's Ancestry Genetic DNA Composition

Although Mackie Lee White Carter's DNA had several matches from West African countries, which provides possibilities to Erma's maternal lineage prior to coming to the Americas during the transatlantic slave trade, there were strong genetic matches to Sierra Leone, Liberia, and Nigeria.

Sierra Leone today is approximately 60% Muslim, 30% indigenous and 10% Christian. Liberia is 85% Christian and 12% Muslim. Nigeria is 58% Christian and 40% of the population adheres to Islam. For Sierra Leone, the two most influential ethnic groups are the Temne and Mende people. The most widely spoken language in Sierra Leone is the Krio language. Liberia includes over 16 ethnic groups, including Kapelle, Bassa, Mano, Gio, Kru, Grebo, Krahn, Vai, Gola, Mandingo, Mende, Kissi, Gbandi, Loma, Fante, Dei, Belleh and Americo-Liberians. Liberia is the settlement of former African American slaves who relocated to Africa because they never thought America would give them fair treatment. The relocation began to take place during President James Monroe's administration, around the year 1821. Nigeria has more than 500 ethnic groups, but the largest are Hausa, Yoruba, Igbo, and Fulani, which make up about 70% of the population.

Erma's maternal ancestors had the strongest genetic ties to Madagascar. Slave ship records show African Americans in general have approximately less than a two percent chance of being descended from natives of Madagascar as a result of the transatlantic slave trade. Therefore, this maternal link to Madagascar is very interesting. It is estimated that approximately 6,000 slaves came from Madagascar on about 17 slave ships that came to the United States (Gates, et al., 2015). Of the hundreds of thousands of slaves who came to the Americas, Erma's maternal line is from Madagascar which is possibly where some of the Southeast Asian ancestry genetic link is coming from based on the DNA results as well. As mentioned earlier, the DNA blood line of Erma did have some Southeast Asian. There is a possibility that centuries earlier, prior to the transatlantic slave trade, Southeast Asians migrated to Madagascar. This theory has not been proven thus far as fact. Madagascar is an island country in the Indian Ocean situated off the coast of Southeast Africa. It is a biodiverse region: over 90% of its wildlife is found nowhere else on

51

earth. Madagascar has over 18 ethnic groups that are tied to the Bantu people, who are believed to have crossed over the Mozambique Channel from East Africa (Gates, et al., 2015).

Figure 4 is a map of Africa, where one can see geographic details of affiliated West African countries and Erma Freeman White's maternal connections.

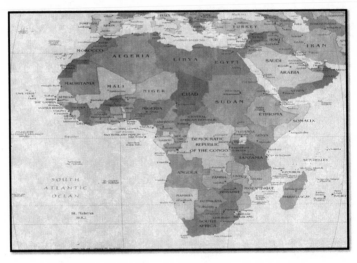

Figure 4. Geographic Details of West African Nations

Sierra Leonne and Liberia stand side by side. Both countries are south of the nation of Guinea. In addition, Liberia is southwest of the country Côte d'Ivoire, also known as the Ivory Coast, which was a French colony formed in 1893. The Ivory Coast achieved independence from France in 1960 (N'Diaye, et al. 2012).

Nigeria is surrounded by three countries: Benin, Niger, and Cameroon. Nigeria is east of Benin, west of Cameroon, and north of Niger.

The transatlantic slave trade is a sad moment in history for the United States as well as for the world. Millions of Africans were transported to the Americas into bondage. Greed was the driving force behind this economic reality. Our families left Africa in slave ships, leaving behind rich cultures, heritages, and traditions. Our ancestors lost our African names only to take the names of their owners in the United States. Stripped of the life of freedom, they could only fight for it through faith and force. We may not be able to know exactly where we came from just prior to the transatlantic slave trade, but thanks to God for DNA and scientific ingenuity, we can come extremely close. DNA scientific analysis is a great tool.

Homecoming

Erma was called to see the Lord on January 23, 1997 due to complications from Alzheimer's Disease. Her funeral service was led by Rev. David L. Jones, her pastor at Good Hope Presbyterian Church in Frierson, Louisiana. The church was packed with family and friends. It is never easy losing the matriarch of the family. She gave all of herself with love and compassion.

And I heard a great voice out of heaven saying, Behold, the tabernacle of God is with men, and he will dwell with them and they shall be his people, and God himself shall be with them and be their God.

And God shall wipe away all tears from their eyes; and there shall be no more death, neither shall there be any more pain; for the former things are passed away. – Revelation 21: 3, 4

Erma is buried next to her husband Jesse in the Good Hope Presbyterian Church cemetery. Erma's legacy is still alive today through all her descendants.

Give me six hours to chop down a tree and I will
spend the first four hours sharpening the axe
                                    Abraham Lincoln

Willie (Bud) Green

Willie "Bud" Green was over six feet tall and a handsome man. He was born on August 15, 1902 in Grand Cane, Louisiana to Billy Green and Hannah Scott Green. The exact date of Bud's birthday for many years was unknown due to lack of documentation. During those times records were not kept as meticulously as they are now. Nevertheless, with the use of Bud's older sisters and the recollection of events from his youth, August 15 is his estimated birthday. Billy and Hannah had six daughters and two sons: Ruby, Lucy, Janie (Pearl), Sarah, Eller, Willie, Birdie Bee (Beatrice), and LD.

Both of Bud's parents died before he was 20 years old. His father died from a disease called pellagra, which is a deficiency disease caused by a lack of nicotinic acid or tryptophan (an amino acid) in the diet (Medline Plus, 2015). Billy's pellagra was linked to the overdependence of corn.

Billy is buried at Good Hope Presbyterian Church in Frierson at the old grave site. The old grave site is now fully covered by the grass and one cannot tell that it was once a grave yard. In the late 1940s, Bud told his children: "the graveyard where my Daddy is buried is totally covered with trees and brush." This is extremely sad because even though Billy Green was born free, the old grave site is the burial ground for many of the former slaves associated with Good Hope Presbyterian Church. In addition, smaller churches that did not have a place to bury their members were allowed to bury their dead at Good Hope. Billy Green was not a member of Good Hope but was buried there. The old grave site is located behind the church's "old" entrance gate, which was used from around the year 1877 until the 1960s. Church members of old could at one time ride a horse-drawn wagon from the south of Frierson, traveling north, to attend Good Hope. By coming this way on this particular road, the first thing one would see is what is today the back of the church. The old grave site today is no longer the property of Good Hope. It is not a situation that Good Hope lost land or did not pay their taxes. Good Hope still today is a strong and viable church. During the late 20th century—after the year 1990—when the land survey was done, it was noted that the old grave yard was not the property of church. There had always been controversy with land surveys associated with Good Hope. According to longtime church members, "every time property markers are correctly drawn for Good Hope, someone pays off a lawyer to take the church land."

Bud's mother Hannah had only one eye. She lost an eye when it was stuck with a rusty barb wire while climbing through a fence. She survived for quite some time with one eye, but she died from blood poisoning from the rust that entered her blood stream. Hannah is buried at Mount Zion Baptist Church in Kingston. Both Billy and Hannah were natives of the Grand Cane area.

As a child, Bud's top priority was survival, and he focused on acquiring food, clothing, and shelter. Education was secondary to survival which is why Bud is said to have only a third grade education. Despite his lack of formal education he was good with numbers. He knew the value of a dollar and hard-earned money.

Bud attended New Friendship Baptist Church in Frierson, Louisiana as an adult. Not far from where New Friendship Baptist Church is located is a town called Lakeville, Louisiana, which is also located in DeSoto Parish. In Lakeville, Bud's ancestors were once property owners. Their land in Lakeville was taken by the white folks in the area because property taxes were not paid on time.

As a teenager through adulthood, Bud showed proficiency in farming, but loved training horses. Throughout the Frierson area, he was known for training domesticated and wild horses. Simply put, Bud was a true cowboy. He kept his horses in a shack that he built.

Survival was difficult. Like his family and neighbors, Bud used the summer and fall to prepare for the winter. Bud would smoke the family's meats in fall in the smoke house so that they would have meat during the winter. Ham was the meat he smoked primarily. For salt pork, he would slice up sections of the hog (pork belly) in small pieces and put it in salt. The salt was placed in layers on top of the meat, which helped cure it, and assisted with keeping the meat lasting longer. For sweet potatoes, Bud covered them with pine straw in his small storage house. He was taught early how to preserve items such as figs, okra, tomatoes, pears, and peaches. These skills were crucial to having a happy winter.

Death of Bud's Brother

Attempting to uncover a sensitive story is not always easy. Bud Green's only brother, LD, was murdered in 1958 when he was around the age of 40. The details of the murder change depending on who tells the story, but here are the two explanations given:

The first account

Living in Gayle, Louisiana at the time, LD Green came home early from a hard day's work to find his wife in bed with another man. Upon surprising the two lovers, the man got up quickly and left the house through a window. Upon exiting the window, the man took a pipe with him, which was used to hold up the window. LD Green gave chase. Upon catching the man, the adulterer struck LD in the forehead and LD fell. Then the man took the pipe and stuck it in LD's head, above his ear.

The second account

According to the second scenario of LD's death, he was set up. A group of men knew that LD was having an affair with a woman and systematically planned to take LD's life. Days before his murder, LD was with a woman other than his wife in an adulterous affair. This woman was said to be the wife of LD's alleged murderer. In addition, this woman who was cheating with LD was the housemaid of Arch and Scribe Frierson. Arch and Scribe Frierson were two powerful brothers in Frierson. Scribe also employed the woman's husband. LD's alleged murderer had allegedly been told by Scribe, "if you can keep yourself alive, I can keep you out of jail." This is sort of an indication the alleged murderer may have been a troublemaker.

On the day of his murder, LD was originally in Shreveport socializing with various men and someone in the group told LD he had better go check on his wife. When he arrived home, LD was beaten to death with a pipe. If this version of his death is true, LD was the third man to be killed because of the Friersons' housemaid. She was a loose woman and brought trouble to any man with whom she became involved.

Regardless of the scenario, LD's murderer spent only a couple of years in jail. Both scenarios are tragic and in the end LD lost his life and Bud lost his only brother.

We Have to Kill What We Eat

There was a time in America when what one had for breakfast, lunch, and supper was based on what you were able to capture in the wild and bring home. Bud was a hunter. It was no big deal even as child for Bud to go out to hunt for animals in the wild for such as rabbit, squirrel, turkey, goose, pig, duck, deer, and raccoon. Bud was also a fisherman. Typical fish in the DeSoto Parish lakes were catfish, buffalo fish, carp, and bass. All of these at one time or another were part of Bud's meals.

One adventurous experience Bud passed down to his family happened sometime in his mid-30s. He was hunting wild hogs. No hunter ever wants to experience a wild hog attempting to attack him. The hunter becomes the hunted. This is exactly what happened to Bud as he walked slowly through the woods that day. He approached several wild hogs. Bud took a quiet aim at the wild hogs and fired his rifle. One of the hogs was hit and several of the other hogs scattered all over the place. In panic, the injured wild hog made eye contact with Bud. The angry wild hog began to chase him. As his adrenaline began to flow at a much higher level than normal, Bud tried but failed to fire a second round with his rifle. Bud dropped the rifle after not being able to take that second shot in time and ran. It was more than likely that Bud wasn't able make that second shot because the wild hog had already started to come at him. With all his God-given physical talents, Bud executed a full sprint in an attempt to save his own life. It was fight or flight. God was on his side this day because as the wild hog gained ground on Bud, he came upon a bent tree. The tree was sloped at probably a 60-degree angle. Bud ran up the bent tree. The injured wild hog got away and Bud had nothing to eat that day because nothing was killed. At least Bud survived another day from the life-threatening experience.

Typically, some animals are off limits within the rural community because they are not considered inedible; however, when one is hungry, it is easy to test those limits. It can sometimes come down to whether one should starve or put something fulfilling in one's stomach. Bud had crossed that road before. Although most others in the family would not try it, it was no big deal for Bud to cook up an armadillo. He knew how to add the proper seasoning and barbeque to an armadillo to perfect a delectable taste. On one occasion, he tricked his wife by giving her some armadillo while she thought it was something else. When she was almost half way done, Bud told her, "you are actually eating armadillo." Senie was very angry and immediately pushed the plate away.

Carpe Diem

In so many cases in the early 20th century, it was implied that blacks couldn't get ahead due to the inferior systems in which they were educated or in which they lived. The separate but equal laws, the black codes, sharecropping as well as the unfair educational system are a few examples of topical discussions among black people who lived during this era.

Bud's older sister Eller was financially prosperous. She married a gentleman named Oliver Tracy. Oliver was born with "it." What is it? It is hard to explain, but he had it. Mr. Oliver Tracy never finished high school, but he was an entrepreneurial genius. Mr. Tracy was a true businessman with the ability to compete with the best on any level and against all odds. In the DeSoto Parish area, there was a high demand for cutting lumber for building and expansion. All of the lumber mills in that area were owned by white men and they were not interested in sharing the wealth. Mr. Tracy refused to be denied an opportunity for family prosperity and was determined to compete with the big boys.

Mr. Tracy built his own saw mill with his bare hands. His production was as competitive and successful as any other saw mill businesses in the area during the time. His business generated revenues which led to the expansion of the business, more employees, land acquisition, and asset purchases. Oliver and Eller Tracy were a wealthy couple. It is said in regards to their personal assets, they had motorcycles, the latest and greatest cars of that year, a jukebox and lots of land, among other possessions.

Although Mr. and Mrs. Tracy were financially independent, farming was still a big part of their lifestyle. Farming was a skill necessary for day-to-day living. In addition, since both had worked farms as children, this skill was not going to waste. Although they stayed busy with farming and their saw mill business, the Tracys had dreams to expand their family. The power couple was blessed with a little boy. The Tracys named their child Billy T. Tracy, after Eller's father. He was a beautiful, healthy boy full of life and potential. All seemed to be going perfectly for them. God had truly blessed them. Although Eller was able to produce breast milk for baby Billy T., it wasn't enough to sustain him. Baby Billy T. constantly cried. Eller tried to supplement breast milk with actual cow's milk. It was commonly said Eller would hold baby Billy T. constantly to keep him quiet, even while cooking. Eller used a wood stove to cook. With the combination holding baby Billy T., exposure to the hot wood stove and the season being the winter, Billy T. became sick. Oliver and Eller took Billy T. to the doctor but a cure was not found. Eller's sister in-law Senie Green, who was knowledgeable of home remedies, was not able get rid of Billy T.'s illness either. Baby Billy T. eventually succumbed to his illness at the age of three months. The doctors determined meningitis the cause of death. Oliver and Eller never fully recovered from this tragedy, and for the rest of her life, Eller blamed herself for her son's death.

The Tracy family tried to cope as well as they could and their business continued to prosper. Oliver eventually closed his business but lived modestly for the remainder of his life. Oliver died on May 27, 1964 from complications of a stroke he had suffered several months earlier. Still farming until his death, Oliver was loading his truck with fertilizer at a local store when he had the stroke and was rushed to the hospital. He originally went to a hospital in Mansfield but they transferred him to Confederate Memorial Hospital in Shreveport. He lived about two months after the stroke. Oliver is buried at Mount Zion Baptist Church in Kingston near his infant son Billy T. Eller outlived Oliver and was left with a lot of assets, particularly land. Even within Frierson's rural area, there are some areas that are more rural than others. Most of the land acquired in DeSoto Parish during this era was when the area was full of large families and packed churches. As job opportunities increased in the Shreveport area as well as the United States for black people, residents moved away from Frierson. Eller did not want to leave Frierson, but she wanted to leave the deep country and live in a more populated area. More people were living within Frierson across the rail road tracks from her property opposite of highway 175.

Eller reached out to her niece, Bud's daughter, for advice on how to relocate from the deep country. Here is where the story can be told differently depending on who tells it. We have heard people in the Frierson community as well as in the Caddo Parish area make statements like: the black man can't get ahead; the white man took the Oliver Tracy's land which was worth millions; the white man took land from Oliver's wife (Eller) for pennies via force; the biggest real estate rip off in American history was what was done by the white man to Oliver Tracy's wife Eller.

It is true that Oliver and Eller Tracy had over 160 acres of land that they owned at one time. Eller being older now and over the age of 60, probably did not have the fight that she once had, and she trusted that the right thing would be done. Here is what happened. Eller's niece, who lived in Frierson, did exactly what Eller requested. She sold the land to folks who were raising hogs, and those folks happened to be white. The land was sold to the highest bidder. Eller's niece had an offer from her brother in-law's distant cousins, who happened to be black, for a much lower amount than the land sold for. Eller's niece had modest financial means and probably did not have all the business savvy needed to make this situation a win-win situation for the Oliver and Eller's estate. Most of Bud Green's children did not agree with the sale of the property, but most family members say their opinions were never sought. Thus, Eller made a big decision without seeking the advice of others.

Prior to Oliver's death, he had sold several small portions of his land to different businessmen as well as to individual families for different purposes. Therefore, the original 160 acres of land had been reduced. At the time of Oliver Tracy's death, Eller was left with approximately 80 acres of land which is still a lot of land. With that said, those 80 acres of Eller's land were sold all at once well below market value. Eller used the proceeds from the sale of her land to purchase less than a quarter of an acre in a different area of Frierson on the other side of rail road tracks close to highway 175, as well as for other purposes. The biggest issue family members had was not the selling of the land, but how the land was sold. The land could have been sold in quarter-acre lots as opposed to all the land in one lump sum. Some family members say the land should never have been sold and that Eller should have just moved to an area of Frierson that was more populated with people. Twenty-twenty is hindsight is true.

Thirty years after the sale of Eller's land, a unique natural gas was discovered in the DeSoto Parish area on her former property. This natural gas is located nowhere else in the world and energy companies want this mineral rights goldmine. If Oliver and Eller were alive today with their original land still in their possession, royalty and mineral rights alone would generate millions of dollars. What is the moral of this story? Land is a great investment, God only made so much of it. Another moral to this story is to seek advice from wise business folks before making huge business deals. Blacks in Frierson preach heavily now: "do not sell your land"; "keep your land"; and pass it down to the next generation. Some of this preaching is directly tied to the Eller Tracy experience, and some of it is tied to the bad sharecropping experience had by many blacks in the area and across the American south. If any generation knows the importance of land ownership, it is the ex-slaves of DeSoto Parish and their descendants, who have not forgotten the tragedies of the American experience. Eller died in May 1988 at the age of 89. She is buried at Mount Zion Baptist Church next to her husband Oliver and infant son Billy T.

Receipt Cleared

Sharecropping on someone else's property is a tough life. It is a tough business on the property owner, but it is a major disadvantage to someone who is looking to climb the American corporate ladder because it was a hard life without a real future in sight. As a family man and during the prime of his life, Bud worked on farms as a sharecropper. Bud would buy the fertilizer and cotton seeds to work Mr. Roach's farm on credit. During this sharecropper arrangement, Bud also purchased groceries on credit from the community store owned by Stallcup. At the end of the year, Mr. Roach would pay Stallcup for all of the bills incurred by Bud associated with living and farming. After Mr. Roach and Stallcup went over all of the expenses, Mr. Roach would pay Stallcup for all of Bud's bills incurred during the year. This business exchange would be worked out between Mr. Roach and Stallcup only. One reason may be because there were probably hundreds of other blacks with similar business arrangements with Stallcup and it was more productive to work out these business deals between store owner and the land owner. In the first year, Bud raised and picked eighteen bales of cotton. Mr. Roach told Bud that during the year he was $35 short and he could not leave his property until that bill was cleared. Bud's family was living on the property. In other words, since Bud owed the property owner $35, he had to continue to work the farm until that debt was paid. In the second year, Bud cleared fewer than eighteen bales of cotton but nevertheless raised a substantial amount of cotton. The second year, Bud still was in debt and could not leave the planation.

In the rural area of DeSoto Parish, it was typical for a kid as young 10 or 11 to drive a car, with or without a driver's license. Bud wanted to buy his son, Lugene, a car when he was around the age of 14 or 15. Bud's son would have to go a great distance to get to school. Lugene would ride a horse from Gravel Point to Frierson approximately seven miles from their home. He would leave his horse at a friend's house who lived in Frierson, and several junior high school students from the neighborhood would walk to school together. Bud wanted to buy his son a car to take "some of the struggle" out of getting an education for his boy by making it easier for him to get to school.

During the third year of sharecropping with Mr. Roach an interesting event occurred. There was a major flood that affected Mr. Roach's plantation. Coincidentally, Bud's farming area on Mr. Roach's property was up on a hill. In addition, Mr. Roach's cows were at the bottom of the hill near the bayou. Mr. Roach told Bud "if you would cut the wires that are fencing in my cows and let them go up on the hill where your cotton is located, I will give you a clear receipt." Mr. Roach also told Bud that he could stay and help other sharecroppers harvest their crops on his property but that would be his choice. Bud agreed to cut the wires of the fence to free the cows who were in the flooding water. Mr. Roach kept his word and gave Bud a clear receipt. Bud was debt free! He immediately left Mr. Roach's planation like a bat out of hell. Bud packed up his wagon and moved from Gravel Point to Friendship. Bud never was able to purchase his son the car he wanted. Lugene would not get his first car until several years later when he found a job in Shreveport. He worked and saved his money. In addition, in the 1960s Lugene bought land for his parents Bud and Senie so they would never have to move around as they did during Lugene's childhood when they moved from plantation to plantation. Photo 2 is a picture of the land Lugene purchased and the home built for Bud and Senie:

Photo 2. Home of Bud and Senie Green

Lugene bought the land from Stallcup, the owner of the community store. Even until this day, descendants of Bud and Senie own that land. It is pretty profound that Bud's descendants have mineral rights to that land and receive money from the natural gas found on that property.

With the fact that slavery was abolished in 1865, it is hard to fathom how still in the 1940s and 1950s, Bud Green and his family were moving from one plantation to another plantation without any sense of security or assets of their own. The entire family was at the mercy of several plantation owners, and living conditions were, for the most part, very poor. Keep in mind from one year to another, Bud would even have his children working the plantation after school to assist with making ends meet. Bud's children mention how it would be miserably cold at night during the winters when they lived in uninsulated rooms. Living conditions were deplorable. They were exposed to the natural elements on one of the plantations and as Bud's children slept in their beds at night, they could look through holes of the ceiling to see the stars and the sky. In addition, within this same plantation, it rained inside their home and they had to place buckets around the house to capture the water. They used quilts made by Senie and heaters to stay warm. Faith, mercy, and the almighty God carried Bud and his family through those challenging times.

Just Controversial

The family of Billy and Hannah experienced such severe financial hardships that one of their daughters, Birdie Bee was reared by extended family in Tulsa, Oklahoma. Birdie Bee visited her siblings in DeSoto Parish occasionally, but she attended school, married and raised a family in Oklahoma. Birdie Bee died in 1993 and is buried in Tulsa. Many of her descendants still reside in that area.

Bud was often described as a little controversial. The Prince Albert tobacco pipe smoking gentleman was said to highly believe in the phrase "spare the rod, spoil the child." This was probably common for most families then. Although the exact details of the situation are unclear, a major disagreement between Bud and one of his daughters escalated. The daughter grew so upset with Bud that she pulled out a knife and stabbed him. The cut was not severe and Bud's injuries were minor, but Bud's inability to control his anger was being passed down to his children. Sadly, he would occasionally apply physical abuse toward his wife. Bud's physical abuse only stopped when one of the sons came of age and grew into a physically large and intimidating young man who said, "Do not ever hit my mother again." After the son's statement, Bud never hit his wife again. The following poem written describes an attempt to express Bud's occasional rage:

As deep as the Holy Bible and as historical as an Egyptian Scroll
The Lord only knows how I have lost control
I said good bye to my father very young, lift this cup to take a
    toast
Tears were in my eyes because I needed him most
Shaken by his lost, hold me while my heart bleed
I have no clue on how to lead
I will do my best; I will give it a try
Looking back, I made mistakes I won't lie
For those I have hurt, forgive me and try to move on
If not, the pain I caused will last long after I'm gone

Grandchildren never saw the physical abuse that Bud's children saw. Bud's grandchildren called him "Papa" and thought the world of him. There is something special about a grandfather having an almighty presence about him that is infused with peaceful love.

Bud's descendants still recount the many plantation stories he shared over the years. This particular story is associated with the Jamie Scott plantation. Bud and his family were living on the Jamie Scott plantation and working on their land as sharecroppers. The details behind the story here again depend on its orator, but the general story pertains to a disagreement between Jamie Scott and Bud. It is not 100% clear if maybe Jamie Scott called Bud "boy" or if there was a "receipt cleared" issue pertaining to how much debt Bud still owed. Nevertheless, one fact that people agree on is that Jamie Scott was on his horse while Bud was standing on the ground when the disagreement occurred. Bud was enraged with Jamie Scott and grabbed him with all the strength in his vibrant body. Jamie Scott was pulled off his horse to the ground and Bud beat him badly. Jamie became angry, but was physically too hurt to respond quickly to Bud's brutality. It was apparent that Jamie wanted to kill Bud, but during the fight neither had weapons on them. Thank God for this. Bud's wife Senie went to Jamie later that day asking for forgiveness and mercy. Jamie told Senie that her family had seventy-two hours to get off his plantation. Bud packed up all the family belongings and was off the plantation within seventy-two hours.

A few times during his youth, Bud would go to churches within the Frierson area and perform mischievous acts. During this period, owning a car of any kind was still a luxury item. The horse wagon was still the primary means of transportation. Prior to entering the evening church services, attendees would harness their horses and wagons to poles. Bud would sneak and unhook the horses from the wagon front side and reconnect the horse to the back side. When church members would finish church services, their wagon was in the front and their horse was in the back of the wagon. He liked to play tricks.

As mentioned earlier, Bud became a horse trainer at an early age. On one occasion, Bud was training horses on a different plantation. On this particular plantation, the rules were horses were not allowed to leave their premises after a certain time. Late one night, Bud went back to that plantation and borrowed their horse. After taking the horse off the plantation "after hours," Bud rode that horse to full capacity. He enjoyed the feeling of speed, adventure, and living on the edge.

Because it was around dusk, Bud did not see the wire ahead of them. At full speed the horse ran into barbed wire fence. It cut its neck profusely and caused the horse to bleed. In sheer panic, Bud took the horse and sewed up the horse's neck with stitches. The injury to the horse was still noticeable, but Bud's medical attention did help the horse to survive. After sewing up the horse's neck that night, Bud took the horse back to the plantation where it belonged. The next morning, the plantation owner of that injured horse said, "I know it was nobody but that Bud who done this." He could never prove it and Bud never confessed.

It was common during this era to catch a train as a means of transportation. Bud was a true adventurer. For passengers who could afford a ride on a passenger train for a fee, one could take a ride that was safe and possibly luxurious. For those who had no money and wanted to get around locally in DeSoto Parish, there was the freight train. During Bud's younger days, it was no big deal to jump on a freight train for free travel. It was dangerous and he was truly putting his life in jeopardy. Exiting a freight train wasn't always easy, especially if the train was still moving quickly. When it came time to jump off, the rider had to consider timing and measuring his velocity all while attempting to land on a relatively soft surface.

With his funds low, Bud decided to hop on a freight train to travel from point A to point B. Bud's timing and measuring the ground surface must have been slightly off that day. As Bud jumped off the freight train upon reaching his destination, he must have slipped. He ended up in a head-first thrust to the ground. The unique thing is that he landed head first into a hole that no one knew was there! As he landed in the ground, the only thing that stopped his entire body from entering a nearby hole was the broadness of his shoulders. As Bud got up from the ground, he was in excruciating pain, but nothing was broken. It took several days for his bruises to heal. Youth was on his side that day. In his later years, he would regularly laugh about this adventure as he shared this experience.

American 100%

Bud Green's father was said to be a light-skinned African American with gray eyes that sometimes appeared to be hazel. It is common to wonder how Bud's father, Billy, inherited that eye color. Somewhere in those genes there is someone of European descent in his blood. The story was that Bud Green's grandfather was a white man. Bud's father was literate and had a title then called "a reader". What was a reader from the black experience during this time? It was a black man who knew how to read during a time when very few blacks knew how to read. Bud's father, Billy, would read the Bible and write in the church ledgers in the Frierson area. He was a record keeper. Billy would walk through the woods late at night after finishing his church ledger reading and writing jobs. These woods were known to have wolves at night. The way Billy kept the wolves at bay was by carrying an ignited pine straw torch which he would light up.

The story passed down from generation to generation was that Bud's grandfather was a white man. When investigating the 1880 United States census, Bud's grandfather Billie Green was listed as living in DeSoto Parish and as a black male. In addition, the census listed Billie Green as a farmer and listed that his parents were from Alabama. Therefore, the story passed down is inaccurate. Our guess is that Billie's father from Alabama might have been a white man. Due to the lack of good record keeping, modern DNA testing is useful.

Bud's son Lugene's DNA was used to answer several

questions. DNA results confirm that the Greens are descendants of slaves, but there is more to this profound family than slavery. The records of our previous owners during the antebellum period treated the Greens as three fifths human and many times would not even mention their names in slave ledgers. We were no different than cattle in their eyes. Thanks to DNA, we can determine if Bud's grandfather Billie was a white man. That information is tied to the male Y chromosome, a unique gene that is passed down from father to son. Bud received it from his father Billy, who got that specific gene from Bud's grandfather Billie. The oldest recorded Green family member, Billie, received that specific gene from his father from Alabama and so on....

It was determined that Bud's lineage most closely matches that of people found in the Lower Guinea region of Africa. Lugene's DNA had matches throughout western Africa, but there was a part of Africa that had more matches than any other western African country. That country was Cameroon. It is highly likely that prior to reaching Alabama as well as the United States, Bud's direct paternal ancestors came from the country of Cameroon. In addition, the Y chromosome proved that Bud's great grandfather, who passed down the Green name, was a black man. The Y chromosome was a direct link to Western Africa and not Europe at all. Although somewhere our white ancestors gave us those grey and hazel eyes, it was not tied to the Green father to father lineage.

Biblically speaking, ancestors from Alabama beget Billie Green, who beget Billy Green, who beget Willie (Bud) Green, who beget Lugene Green, who beget Marvin Green, who beget Marley Green. Only one of Bud's biological sons had another son. Therefore, Bud Green's name is in the hands of his great grandson Marley Green, who now lives in Los Angeles, California.

Sunset

Later in Bud's life, he became more dedicated to the Lord. As an older man, he became a deacon at New Friendship Baptist Church. Bud truly believed in his heart in the book of John chapter 3, verse 16, which says: *For God so loved the world that He gave His only begotten Son, that whoever believes in Him shall not perish, but have eternal life.*

Bud died on July 16th, 1986 from lung cancer. The doctors thought part of the cancer came from asbestos exposure and partly from smoking tobacco. As a young father of small children, Bud worked in Michigan for a short time building ships. Later, that type of work was found to have given those workers asbestos exposure.

Bud currently has over 40 direct descendants still alive today. Bud is buried at Mount Zion Baptist Church in Kingston, Louisiana next to his daughter Ruby Green Brown.

*Until lions tell their tale, the story of the hunt
will always glorify the hunter.*

African Proverb

Senie Winters

Senie Winters was born on February 4, 1904 in Stonewall, Louisiana to Bob (Robert) Winters and Easter Brown Winters. Both Bob and Easter were first generation free born Americans, born after the Emancipation Proclamation. Bob was born in 1868 and Easter was born in 1871. They had a total of seven children—four boys and three girls—named Abb, Hopkin, Bob Jr., Brazzie, Neva, Betsy, and Senie Winters. Senie was not the baby in the family, but she was the baby girl. All were born in DeSoto Parish in the Stonewall area. Bob Winters Jr. was called to see the Lord early and died around the year 1918 at the age of 11. Senie's sister, Betsy, was said to be a recluse, perhaps because of the complications she suffered as an albino. Some of the affiliated symptoms she dealt with could have been crossed eyes, sensitivity to light, and involuntary rapid eye movements. Being different from one's peers is not easy in the 21st century, and certainly not in a small community in the early 20th century.

Both Bob and Easter were born right in the heart of the reconstruction era, which was at its peak from 1865 to 1877. As children, these two were just innocent little children, playful and full of hope. Probably as children these two were unaware of some of the federal laws that had been passed that were affecting them. Prior to the assassination of Abraham Lincoln, there were subtle indications that Lincoln wanted all men to be created equal, regardless of their race, creed or color and a plan of action for newly freed slaves. With President Andrew Johnson taking over after Lincoln, it appears Johnson had extreme difficulty pleasing Northerners, Southerners, whites, blacks, Republicans, and Democrats simultaneously. In addition, President Johnson was not able to make both political parties content on decisions being made related to businesses, capitalism, fair free trade and infrastructure (Ash, at al,, 2012).

As a little girl Easter Brown Winters was a member of St. Matthew Baptist Church in Stonewall, Louisiana. St. Matthew's was founded on June 14, 1881 under the leadership of Reverend J.S. Christian. The church moved to Stonewall in October 1952 under Reverend J. Cawthran. Today, St. Matthew's is in its same location of 3799 Highway 3276, Stonewall, LA.

Love can conquer greed in the long term, but change is never easy. Senie's parents were married on January 14, 1893 in DeSoto Parish. Bob and Easter's story is a true love tale that is woven with intricate details of sacrifice for one another. First Corinthians chapter 13, verses 4 through 8 describes love to the utmost:

Love is patient, love is kind. It does not envy, it does not boast, it is not proud.
It does not dishonor others, it is not self-seeking, it is not easily angered, it keeps no record of wrongs. Love does not delight in evil but rejoices with the truth.
It always protects, always trusts, always hopes, always perseveres.
Love never fails. But where there are prophecies, they will cease; where there are tongues, they will be stilled; where there is knowledge, it will pass away.

Easters and Bob Winters' love was pure, committed, kind, and with a mission. Through the mountains and the valleys of their life together, they persevered. Raising their seven children and farming their crops were not easy responsibilities. Providing food, clothing, and shelter wasn't always simple, but they worked together as a couple. Easter's mother Abb Powers Brown was said to have been a slave in the state of Georgia prior to moving to DeSoto Parish after the Civil War ended. It is not certain if Abb is short for Abbie (Abby) or Abigail, but Easter called her mother Abb. With the history in America of not acknowledging marriages of blacks during the antebellum period, it is extremely pleasing to find a marriage license for a family member less than 30 years after slavery was abolished. Figure 5 is an image of Bob and Easter Winters' marriage license.

Figure 5. Bob and Easter Winters' Marriage License

As seen in Figure 5, the actual marriage license states that Bob and Easter were married under Minister Simpson. Also, there were three witnesses. There must have been a feeling of euphoria between the two when they realized that they were being treated the same as all other marriages with the state of Louisiana's acknowledgement and authorization. Jumping the broom was not necessary anymore; passing down wills and assets was now a probable situation.

This may have been a short-lived dream due to what happened three years after Bob and Easter's marriage. With the Plessy versus Ferguson court case, which was decided on May 18, 1896, by a seven-to-one majority, the U.S. Supreme Court, approved the controversial "separate but equal" doctrine for assessing the constitutionality of racial segregation laws (Esty, 105). Freed American blacks' rights were enforced through the laws of the 13th, 14th, and 15th amendments of the United States Constitution. The Plessy versus Ferguson court case was the first major change to question the meaning of the 14th amendment which in 1868 granted citizenship to all persons born or naturalized in the United States (Schafer, at al., 501). This 14th constitutional amendment included former slaves who had just been freed after the Civil War. Louisiana legislation had already approved one particular segregation law prior to the Plessy versus Ferguson ruling, such as the "Louisiana Separate Car Act" of July, 1890 (Schafer, at al., 1997).

The intent behind this state law was to provide "equal but separate accommodations for the white and colored races" on lines running in the state. The tough part to recognize here is that not only was the state of Louisiana enforcing these laws of separate but equal, but now the United States government was enforcing them nationally. Again, all Easter and Bob had was each other, God, and LOVE. Only God and love could overcome such an insurmountable uphill battle. Abraham Lincoln said *"a house divided against itself cannot stand."* The ratification of Louisiana Separate Car Act and Plessy versus Ferguson court case is basically saying the hell to what honest Abe thought (Ivers, at al., 2012).

Slave Auction in Georgia

Oral traditions were a big part of the Winters family legacy. Depending on the person discussing them, the details of some stories may differ slightly, but the crux of the story stays the same. In this case, what might be debatable is the location of the event, but one fact passed down that stays the same is Abb Powers Brown's nine children were all sold during a slave auction.

In an incident that is believed to have occurred in the state of Georgia, the slave owner of Abb and her children had liabilities and debts that far exceeded his assets and income. He had to make a tough decision in order to keep his business profitable. The slave owner decided to sell Abb's nine children. Keep in mind during this time blacks were considered no more than only property. During the U.S. census, slave owners were not required to list their slaves by name. For representation in Congress, Abb and her children were only considered nameless three-fifths humans. Basically, every five slaves would be counted as three people: partially human assets, similar to cattle.

Prior to the auction, the word was spreading that the selling of people was going to take place on the plantation. The night before the auction, Abb begged and begged her owner not to sell her children. Her pleas fell on deaf ears. Below is a poem that describes only minutely how Abb must have felt:

Such a beautiful child
Such a happy child
Unaware of life's struggles
True innocence at the inception
A soul of purity
A child of God but with limits on true freedom
With limits on true freedom

One by one, all of Abb's nine children were sold. Each sale left Abb heartbroken to the core, devastated to the last.... Too weak to walk or stand.... So hurt, no sounds could be heard. All her feelings had been pierced, her sight now blinded by what was reality and what was not. Now as she touched, she felt nothing. Abb was both physically and mentally deteriorated. Abb never recovered from this tragedy. After the slaves in America were set free, Abb moved to DeSoto Parish, Louisiana. She had one more child post-civil war fathered by Caesar Brown. That child would be Easter Brown Winters, who was born free!

Childhood

Senie was named after her paternal grandmother, who was born in Alabama around the year 1845 and was married to Dewitt Winters. Dewitt was also born in Alabama around the year 1825. Dewitt and Senie Winters had four children: James, Betsy, William, and Bob. In 1910, Bob and Easter were living in DeSoto Parish, Louisiana in Chenier. By 1920, they were still living in the same area, in Stonewall.

As a child, Senie demonstrated a lot of academic talent. She had the ability to use inductive and deductive reasoning to solve complicated problems in school. Studying came naturally to her, and she stood out among her peers. Although she finished school up through the junior high level, her ability to solve problems was apparent from the beginning. After her teenaged years, but prior to marriage, Senie tutored the white children whose homes she cleaned. As a child, she attended Stonewall Elementary and Junior High. The school system was tied to the church. Schools were small rooms with wooden benches and a blackboard. The church was crucial in the establishment of children's education.

The time period tied to Senie's childhood and adolescence was one during which gender roles affected many aspects of children's lives. Males had their roles and female had their roles. Adults attempted to make those roles that seemed not to be gender-specific as black and white as possible. For example, most females had jobs like maids or babysitters. In addition, males had all the physically challenging occupations that often required them to work outdoors. It had to be a truly humbling experience to Senie as a young girl to accept the fact that, with all her God-given talent, she had to be confined to certain roles.

As a little girl, Senie assisted her father, Bob Winters, working on the crops of his land. She had chores affiliated with the gathering of the crops. Her brothers performed the plowing work, and Senie and her sisters were responsible for gathering the crops. The crops the family harvested included but were not limited to peanuts, beans, tomatoes, carrots, potatoes, corn, watermelon, onions, walnuts, pecans, collard greens, mustard greens and turnip greens. Cotton picking was not off limits to anyone either.

In regards to her faith, Senie attended her mom's church, St. Matthew's, as a child, but later in life—after teenage years but before marriage—she became a member of Providence Baptist Church. Providence Baptist Church was organized on May 20th, 1868 by Reverend James Christian. It was remodeled in May 1949 by Reverend J.D. Pennywell. Providence Baptist Church is also in Stonewall, Louisiana, approximately three miles east of St. Matthew Baptist Church, but on the north side of the street. After marriage, Senie joined St. Rest Baptist Church in Frierson.

During Senie's teenaged years, she started experimenting with snuff. Her favorite brand was Garrett Snuff Number 4. Number 4 was the highest notch, or the strongest snuff. Later in life, Senie smoked a pipe, using Prince Albert tobacco. The snuff experience was common for many people during this period.

Courting

Who are you courting? The question may seem a little archaic now, but during the early 20th century, parents would ask their children that question. The term "dating" became common several decades later. There is a subtle difference between courting and dating. Courtship stems from the belief that the two people have no physical contact at all—no touching, no hand-holding, no kissing—until the two took their marriage vows. This is what parents of the early 20th century hoped and prayed for in their children's lives. Of course, parents could never control their children's human nature. One cannot help who he or she is attracted to and some of the natural urges within. Nevertheless, parent did their best to control their children and who they courted. Over time, Senie would better understand the complexities of building relationships and courting. In her later years, one of her commonly mentioned "old sayings" about men was "if you want to pull down a man, put a beautiful woman in front of him."

Senie's marriage to Bud was not her first marriage, but it was Bud's first marriage. She had been married before to a gentleman named Albert Evans. Senie and Albert married on April 11, 1931, when Senie was 27 years old. When Senie married Albert, she already had two children. Their names were Wilson Lee and Bob Artist. Wilson Lee and Bob Artist were not Albert's biological children. They were born in the years 1926 and 1928, respectively. The actual marriage between Albert and Senie did not last long, and within a couple of years they were divorced.

Some of the details of how Bud and Senie originally met are not known, but they crossed paths on different occasions and at various functions in the Frierson/Gravel Point area. The type of events they attended individually in the Frierson/Gravel Point area were church-related events or functions hosted by acquaintances or family members. Bud had a romantic side. Although he could neither read nor write, he knew Senie was a smart woman and would be impressed by receiving a letter that he had written. Bud had his friend Will Williams write Senie a series of letters on his behalf. All the time and effort Bud put forth sending those letters to Senie truly impressed her.

Figure 6 is a copy of Senie and Bud's marriage license.

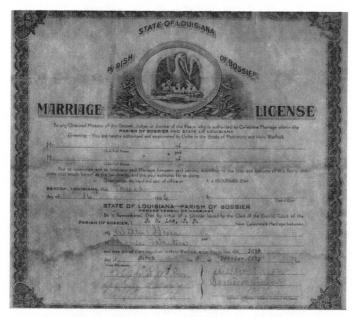

Figure 6. Marriage License of Willie and Senie Green

They officially married on March 16th, 1946 in Parish of Bossier, Bossier City, Louisiana. Senie Winters' new name became Senie Green.

Bud became the active father of both Wilson Lee and Bob Artist. Together, Senie and Bud had six more children. Their six biological children were Lugene, Elizabeth, Leeman, Ella, Ruby, and Lucille. Two more of their children died at birth. Senie and Bud reared eight children together, all of whom lived well into adulthood.

Education

The balancing act of educating your children and protecting them can be a complicated feat. Under the DeSoto Parish class system, it was clearly known that white men and white women could call a black male "boy" regardless of his age. However, black males were required to call white people sir, Mister, Mrs. or ma'am. In addition, not even a little white girl was required to greet or call black adult females as Miss or Mrs. Blacks could not look white people directly in their eyes. People could read your eyes, and your eyes always told how you really felt. This silent rule was passed down from the time of slavery. When slaves hated to work those fields for no pay, they could look their master in the eyes without saying a word, and those looks alone could indicate a form of rebellion or reveal the unpleasant truth that the slaves did not want to perform those duties. The easy way for slaves not to show how they really felt was to just look at the ground, never looking master, overseer, or any whites in the eyes.

When one of Senie's more rebellious daughters was around the age of five or six, she was allowed to play with a neighbor from down the road, who was a white girl. The two children were playing under the porch of Senie's house. Senie's daughter said, "my mother is older than your mother, so why do you call my mother Senie and I have to call your mother Mrs.? You better call my mother Mrs. Senie or I will call your mother by her first name too."

Although it will never be known what was discussed at the white family's dinner table that night, the little white girl never came back to Senie's house again to visit. Senie did tell her daughter at the Greens' dinner table that night to stop talking so much or she would get into trouble. This particular daughter of Senie just happened to have been born just two months apart from Emmett Till. Emmett Louis Till was a black teenager who was lynched in Money, Mississippi while visiting from Chicago during the summer of 1955 after flirting with a white woman. Emmett was only 14 years old when he was murdered.

Senie had to know the temperaments of all her children, and she was no doubt able to decide how much freedom to give each child in regards to visiting family, neighbors, and friends. Senie made it easy on herself and her family; she rarely ever let her children go visit anyone.

In the early years of education for Senie's children, they attended schools within the DeSoto Parish. There were only a few grade and middle schools, including New Zion, Gravel Point, and Friendship schools. All of these schools were directly affiliated with the churches that shared their names. Malcolm X said, "Education is our passport to the future, for tomorrow belongs to the people who prepare for it today" (Shabazz, et al., 54). The church was the key to educating the community and making progressive change.

Elementary schools were grades one through six. All six levels were in one room. Only benches separated one grade from another. Assignments were broken up by grade levels and students were placed in different sections of the small classroom. One might ask, how did the teachers manage all these different grades in one classroom? It was not easy, but one reason, according to former students at least, is that the teachers were short-tempered and mean as hell. A teacher might, at the drop of dime, pull out a belt or a ruler and hit a student with it. Good behavior was a requirement with no exceptions. The unfortunate side of this system was that some teachers were not always fair in how they enforced this punishment. Certain children would have less favor from teachers and were more likely to endure spankings for offenses for which other children were not punished.

Teachers were not always the most knowledgeable educators. Although Grambling College did educate our best and brightest teachers in the north Louisiana region, those well-trained educators often left for larger cities to earn higher pay. This was the case even though Grambling College urged its graduates to go back to their communities to teach. Grambling College had established a program to provide general training for teachers who had no experience. In this program, a student could come to Grambling College and get some general knowledge about how to teach. Within a year, the general teacher education program would issue a teaching certificate to the newly minted teacher assistant. This particular program was for certifying teachers, but it also gave basic training in how to teach and how to help children learn. The program was helpful, but DeSoto Parish still needed more qualified and certified teachers to educate our young during that time.

Pharmacy in the Woods

Decades prior to the establishment of a national healthcare system by the Health Care Financing Administration (HCFA) or the Centers for Medicare & Medicaid Services (CMS), home remedies were widely used for various illness for people of less fortunate financial means. Senie's community believed in her recommended home cures for their children's health problems.

Since pesticides were not commonly used on the crops eaten and foods were not processed as they are today during that era, many illnesses that exist in the 21st century were not prevalent in the late 19th and early 20th centuries, but other illnesses were of great concern to the people who were alive at that time. Therefore, the aphorism (profound statement) "an ounce of prevention is worth a pound of cure" applies in any era. Of course, people with various illnesses should consult their physicians prior to trying Senie's home remedies. Still, her remedies were proven to work on people within the DeSoto Parish community during her lifetime:

Common Cold Remedies

(#1) – Boil pine straws and cow dung (tied in a towel or rag) in water and drink it.

(#2) – Adults drink two tablespoons of castor oil every four to five hours until the system is entirely flushed out.

(#3) – Pronounced "Outin" within the community, this remedy was for chest colds and was composed of a soft flannel material, tallow (cow fat), which was pronounced "tahla," and Vicks Vapor Rub, which was called "Vick-sav" within the community. The Vicks salve was rubbed into the cloth and then placed on the ill person's chest. The flannel was dipped in the warm tallow first. The ailing person slept with the cloth on his or her chest overnight.

(#4) – Boil a mint plant in water and drink it, mostly during the winter time to make one feel good. The mint plant, which commonly grew on trees in the woods of DeSoto Parish, is also used to make the flavor within chewing gum.

(#5) – Mullein was a plant that also grew freely in DeSoto Parish back yards. It was made into a tea by boiling the plant in water and drinking it. (On a separate and side note, mullein was also used to make hair grease or scalp moisturizer.)

Note: It is not recommended that people mix one cold remedy with another.

Internal Worms (children) - Take green garlic from the garden, and mash it with sugar into a powdered candy. Give the mixture to your children with turpentine for four to seven days for the cure.

On a separate note, the federal government had rations during World War II, and that food rationing program gave out sugar stamps, among other items, to the poor. Sugar stamps were ration throughout the United States, including DeSoto Parish. Senie was therefore able to purchase sugar for free for a period of time.

Stepping on a rusty nail - Beat the foot with a hard object until the spot where the nail entered the foot opens up and bleeds. Beating the injured spot until it bleeds draws the poisonous rust out of the foot. After beating the foot until it bleeds, place the foot in warm salted water. Soaking the foot in Epsom salts is also a good way to prevent infection.

Stomachaches – One spoon of salt or baking soda eases stomachaches.

Burned Skin

(#1) – Place goose dung and cow fat inside a cloth and apply the cloth to the burned skin.
(#2) – Grind pine cones into a powder. Combine water and the ground pine cones into a paste, then apply the paste to the burned skin to heal it.

Again, for 21st century cures, consult your physician before trying any of these remedies.

Phytolacca Americana, a poisonous plant that grows in the woods of DeSoto Parish, was commonly known as poke salad, or, in Senie's community, "Poke Sally." People used it in collard greens to increase the amount of greens prepared if you had a large family to feed. The poke salad had to be boiled and squeezed to be effective because of its toxicity. White people within the community would buy Poke Sally from Senie. When money was hard to come by and doctors were not available, families had to improvise using what was available to them.

Taking Advantage of an Opportunity

Easter Brown Winters's family was well connected in the Stonewall area of DeSoto Parish. At the turn of the 20th century, the Brown extended family took advantage of opportunities presented. In the 1910 United States census, Robert Winters mentioned that he could read as well as write. In addition, Robert revealed that he paid a mortgage for land that he owned and on which he farmed. Fred Brown, who was believed to be related to Easter Brown, purchased 180 acres of land with Robert Winters in Stonewall. Fred Brown mentioned in the 1910 census that he could not read and could not write. In addition, Fred Brown declared that he owned land that was mortgage free. Figure 7 is a copy of the transaction record for the land purchased by Fred Brown and Robert Winters.

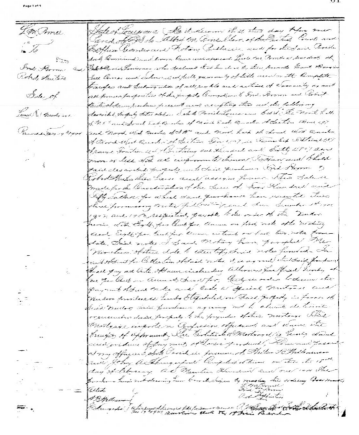

Figure 7. Land transaction—Fred Brown and Robert Winters

Brown and Winters purchased 180 acres of land from Luke M. Powel of DeSoto Parish for $450. The transaction was recorded in the DeSoto Parish Court House on February 19th, 1901. In the 21st century, in the year 2016, the area once owned by Fred Brown includes a street called Brown Road, named after descendants of Fred Brown. This transaction is an example of one family working together to build economic independence within the family structure. Fred Brown and his wife Martha Brown would eventually pass this land down to their son, Fred Brown, Jr. Coincidentally, Fred and Martha Brown had a son named Caesar Brown which was also the name of Easter Brown Winters's father.

1922 Ford for Family Land

In the 1920 U.S. Census, Bob Winters, a farmer, stated that he owned land that was free and clear of a mortgage. Bob Winters was, therefore, a true real estate mogul, with two transactions alone affiliated with land purchases, totaling 220 acres. Bob Winters purchased an additional 40 acres of land in 1903. When a man marries a woman, he has already anticipated plans for his family. In the Holy Bible, Jeremiah 29:11 reads: "'For I know the plans I have for you,'" declares the Lord, plans to prosper you and not to harm you, plans to give you hope and a future." Bob Winters had plans to prosper his family. Bob had a vision to prosper, give hope, and provide a bright future to his wife and children. He wanted and needed land to prosper his family, and Bob wanted to fulfill his dream independent of extended family. To achieve this goal, he and Easter made a business decision; they purchased their own land. Figure 8 is the record of the actual purchase of their land together.

Figure 8. Record of Land Purchase by Bob Winters

The transaction shown in Figure 8 is a record of the 40 acres of land purchased by Bob Winters from D.E. Nicholson, a Caddo Parish resident. Bob Winters purchased the land for

$63.75, with a down payment of $1.00. The remaining balance of $62.75 was due under the terms of a promissory note. Recorded in the DeSoto Parish Court House on January 22nd, 1903, this transaction was the beginning of Bob Winters' true independence from the Jim Crow south and the despicable sharecropping system. Sometime between 1910 and 1920, Bob and Easter Brown Winters paid off this mortgage.

If anything ever tested Bob and Easter Winters' marriage, it was an event associated with a 1922 Ford. Several people tell the story in different ways, but in the end it is another sad American story with one thing in common: someone took land away from someone else. Bob and Easter Winters, like any couple, wanted the finer things in life. To that end, they took a gamble. At that time, Americans were transitioning with full momentum to new modes of transportation. The horse and buggy was slowly becoming a thing of the past, replaced by the faster and more efficient automobile. Bob wanted that 1922 Ford badly. Easter was not as thrilled about the 1922 Ford as Bob. As previously mentioned, Bob and Easter owned 40 acres of land in Stonewall. The land was acquired from hard work and intense labor. This land was earned from years of savings and sacrificing. Their land purchase was based on always having a place to lay your head and farming to produce your own food for total self-reliance and the possibility of free trade. Owning your own land always gave one the belief that you could produce crops that could potentially leave your farm and make it to the open market. Land provided tremendous hope. The Winters' land was located across the street, approximately a quarter mile or so west, from St. Matthew Baptist Church on Stonewall Road.

Bob and the unidentified white man who owned the Ford worked out a deal. We will call this person Taker. Bob could not afford the 1922 Ford, and financing it via a personal loan from Taker was Bob's best way of obtaining that car. Taker had Bob sign an agreement that if Bob defaulted on the payment of the loan for the car, Taker had the right to take Bob's 40 acres. It has been said that Bob Winters could not have comprehended the magnitude of the transaction he was about to sign. The 1922 Ford Model T was over five years old at the time of purchase and was not working very well. The useful life of the car was practically over when the transition between Bob and Taker occurred, around the year 1927 or early 1928.

Easter was not involved at all in the transaction between Taker and Bob. She did not work with Bob as an advisor in this deal, though she was much smarter academically than her husband. Both Bob and Easter could read and write, but Easter was known to be very good with arithmetic also. Bob signed the loan agreement with Taker by placing the letter "X" for his signature in the area where his signature was required.

Over time, Bob defaulted on his payment to Taker. Taker made Bob and Easter get off their land. Anger and sadness overwhelmed them both. Neither Bob nor Easter could believe their worst nightmare was coming true. Misbelief, regret, embarrassment, loss of hope and faith, loss of security, and hatred all happened simultaneously in one moment. As they walked off their land, Easter went to live on another plantation owned by a different white man and Bob went to live on a separate plantation. They never divorced, but their marriage was never the same.

Bob's unwise decision overwhelmed Easter. The system at the time did not work well on behalf of blacks, and to fight the system based on the legality of various business transactions against a white man could cost you your life. Bob would have a stroke not long after losing their land. Senie found Bob face down on the front lawn suffering from the stroke. Senie picked up her father Bob and nursed him back to fairly good health using all the home remedies she knew to help him recover from his stroke. He lived about a year after Senie took responsibility for his health. Bob died in 1929.

This tragic property transaction occurred on what is today called "Country Place", which is a subdivision in the Stonewall area that is still across the street from St. Matthew Baptist Church, less than a quarter of mile west of the church. It must be noted that in the year of 1929–1930, Bob Winters's son Brazzie begged Taker to renegotiate that loan and give the family another chance to get back their land, but his request fell on deaf ears. Today, that exact spot where the 40 acres that were taken away from Bob and Easter Winters was sold by the descendants of Taker in over 25 individual lots into what is now a beautiful subdivision in the Stonewall area. God bless America!

Easter was said to be a dark complexioned attractive woman who stood about five feet ten inches tall. She was also said to be a full figured woman of approximately one hundred forty or so pounds in her prime. As she started to get up in age, she became weak and less mobile. Easter died in 1952 at the estimated age of 82. Even later in life Easter talked about how difficult it was, even 20 years later, to know that the deed to land with her name on it was now in the hands of the white man. Easter is buried at Providence Baptist Church in Stonewall, Louisiana.

This land transaction pertaining to the 1922 Ford occurred approximately 90 years ago. The same land currently has mineral rights associated with it for amounts that exceed over half a million dollars. We should all redefine what a true sacrifice is. If one can bless his or her descendent generations after they have passed on, a major sacrifice was made somewhere. In addition, some families should really look deeply into how their wealth was accumulated and ask God for forgiveness for oppressing others to gain what is believed to be the finer things in life. If greed is driving you, you will fall away from God's will in the end. What good is it to buy all these great assets in America only to lose your soul in the afterlife?

Ancestry Composition

Ever since Abb Powers, Senie Green's maternal grandmother, was a slave, the family has viewed themselves as Americans. Because of separate but equal laws, black codes, and the civil rights movement, our family has been separately classified as Negro, Colored, Black, and African American, along with a lot of other descriptions. Based on our history, we came to America on slave ships during the transatlantic slave trade.

With so many rumors, we were curious about two things: did we have any Native Americans in our family tree, and what part of Africa did we come from prior to coming to America? Let me share with you some of the possibilities and rumors. For purposes of explaining genetic ties and ending confusion, I will call Senie Green what her grandchildren called her: "Dear Dear," as if they were saying "mother dear" twice very quickly.

Dear Dear's paternal grandmother, Senie Winters (wife of Dewitt Winters), was rumored to be a full-blooded Native American. The specific tribe is unknown. When obtaining the census records, her race was mentioned as black. This does not mean our first Senie didn't have Native American blood, but maybe what was passed down was not quite right, not full blooded, or not recorded accurately by the census employee.

Dear Dear had high cheekbones and brown eyes. With her unique features, the family used oral traditions and the sight of Dear Dear's physical features to justify the family having some Native American ancestry in our family tree. We wanted to end all the Native American blood rumors as well as end the curiosity of what part of Africa our ancestors lived in prior to the coming to America. We used the DNA of one of Dear Dear daughters, Ella Deloise Green White, to solve these mysteries.

Figure 9 is a chart that summarizes what we learned regarding their line:

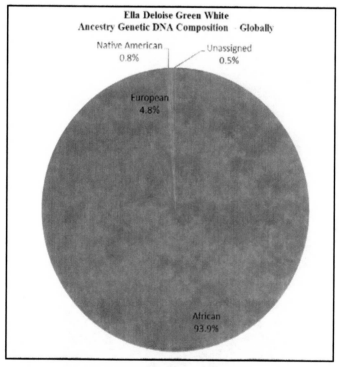

Figure 9. DNA Summary: Ella Deloise Green White's Ancestry Genetic DNA Composition

Based on Figure 9, we had about 1% Native American in our DNA. It was not a large amount, but there was some. In addition, we were 5% European and 94% African. We were not able to confirm if the 5% European blood in our DNA is tied to the slave master who at one time owned our ancestors.

Ella's DNA was also able to tie Dear Dear's ancestors to specific regions of Africa. A great cultural mystery. The results show that prior to being brought over on slave ships, our genetic ties were heavily linked to the Upper Guinea area of Africa which runs from Senegal to Southwest Mali to Northwest Liberia. It was also noted that within the Upper Guinea area, our DNA was tied to two countries more strongly than any other: Senegal and Guinea. See Figure 10 and Figure 11.

Flag of Senegal

Figure 10. Flag of Senegal

Flag of Guinea

Figure 11. Flag of Guinea

The two flags are very similar. Both use the same colors of red, yellow and green. Both have the yellow strip in the middle. In contrast, the first stripe of the Senegalese flag is green and the last stripe is red. The stripes are reversed on the Guinean flag. The Senegalese flag has a green star in the center of its yellow stripe.

The Africa to America DNA results revealed to us that the unique gene passed down from mother to daughter was a direct link to an African woman who had that same gene. Abb's mother passed down that gene to her; Abb passed it down to Easter; Easter passed it down to Dear Dear; and Dear Dear passed it down to her four daughters. Using Ella Deloise Green White's DNA, we were able to determine that our African nationalities prior to being brought over on the slave ships were Senegalese and Guinean.

DNA is pretty awesome. Ella Deloise Green White's DNA showed us that there were also matches to other Americans who were unknown blood relatives within the United States. Many were African Americans but several families tied to Ella's DNA were not. Could some of those matches be tied to the descendants of Abb's nine children who were sold at the slave auction? Thus far, we have not been able to confirm this.

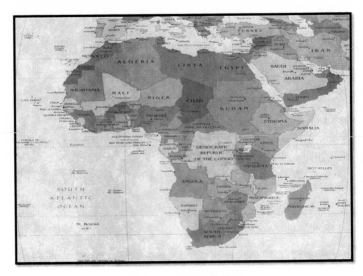

Figure 12. Map of Africa

Senegal and Guinea are most likely where Dear Dear's ancestors came from prior to the slave trade to the Americas. Senegal is south of Mauritania, west of southern Mali and north of western Guinea. Guinea is south of Senegal, north of both Sierra Leone and Liberia. Liberia is the settlement of former African American slaves who relocated back to Africa because they never thought America would end their discriminatory practices. The relocation took place under President James Monroe's administration around the year 1821 (Library of Congress, 2010).

Guinea's geography also lies west of the Ivory Coast and south of Mali. Both Senegal and Guinea are on the coast of West Africa. Senegal's official language is French, but it has a wide variety of ethnic groups where several languages are widely spoken. The Wolof are the largest single ethnic group in Senegal and makes up about 43% of the population; the Fula and Toucouleur ethnic groups are the second largest and about 24%; the Serer ethnic group is the third largest and makes up approximately 15%; the Jola is 4% and the Mandinka is 3%; The remainder makes up of about 9% combined with the Maures, Soninke, Bassari and many smaller ethnic groups. Today, 94% of the Senegal population is Muslim and about 5% are Christian (Our Africa, 2015).

Similar to Senegal, Guinea's official language is also French but other common languages spoken are Pular, Maninka, Susu, Kissi, Kpelle and Loma (Ethnologue, 2015). The Guinea population is comprised of approximately 24 ethnic groups. The Fulas is around 40% of the population and are mostly found in the Futa Djallon region. The Mandinka, also known as Mandingo or Malinké, comprise 26% of the population and are mostly found in eastern Guinea concentrated around the Kankan and Kissidougou prefectures. Guinea population is approximately 85% Muslim, 8% Christian and the remaining 7% practicing indigenous religious beliefs (Countries and Their Cultures, 2015).

Sunset

On Sunday, August 12, 1979, Dear Dear died. Her obituary contains the scripture Psalms 23:4: "Yea, though I walk through the valley of the shadow of death, I will fear no evil; thy rod and thy staff they comfort me." Dear Dear gave her life to Christ at Providence Baptist Church and later united with St. Rest Baptist Church where she remained a faithful servant of Christ until her death. Dear Dear is buried at Providence Baptist Church near her maternal ancestors and siblings. Heaven took our angel and our genius.

Love

Love will always conquer greed. In the 1870 United States census, both spouses Dewitt and Senie Winters stated they could neither read nor write. Both were slaves at one time in their lives under the control of the segregated class system of white supremacy. More than 145 years later, over 80% of Dear Dear and Bud Green's grandchildren have attended college. In addition, more than 40% of Dear Dear and Bud Green grandchildren have earned college degrees. It was Dear Dear and Bud's greatest joy when one of their daughters, Elizabeth Green Mitchell, finished college. This is a testament to the power of God and Jesus Christ our savior. America is the land where dreams come true. Love and ideas never die; they only reinvent themselves and are carried out with the assistance of God, His angels, and His divine intervention, to be fulfilled by those who continuously walk by faith and not by sight.

Faith is put to the test when the situation is most difficult.

> *Mahatma Gandhi*

Jesse White

Named after his paternal grandfather, Jesse White was born in Frierson, Louisiana on June 20, 1915 to Hezekiah White Sr. and Alfair Lee Jones White. Although he was very close with and had a deep love for both his parents, Jesse had a true bond with his mother, Mrs. Alfair. Alfair was born on the 8th of March 1890 to Mr. David Jones and Mrs. Patsy Pierre Jones of Frierson, Louisiana. Mrs. Alfair was the ninth of eleven sisters and brothers. Baptized in August of 1906 by Reverend J.J. Fuller at the Antioch Baptist Church, she later changed her membership to Good Hope Presbyterian Church after her marriage in 1913. Good Hope Presbyterian Church was where her uncle, Fortune Pierre, was pastor. He was the first black ordained pastor and he served in that role for 42 years. Mrs. Alfair was an active member of Good Hope for 73 years. She was the first musician at the church, and for a period of time, she was president of the choir and Women's Work as well as a Sunday school teacher at Good Hope. Mrs. Alfair was a true leader and was aggressive in meeting personal objectives and goals. These characteristics were passed down to her son Jesse.

Jesse attended Frierson Elementary for grades one through eight, and attended high school at DeSoto Parish Training School. As a young man, he worked on his parent's farm. Jesse was converted and baptized at Good Hope Presbyterian Church in 1925 at the age of ten. One of Jesse's favorite sayings was "You never miss your water until your well run dry."

103

Religion

Based on church records, immediately after the Civil War, circa 1866, Good Hope Presbyterian Church survived in DeSoto Parish thanks to three key people. All of the white members had left Frierson because the Frierson area and country were still in disarray. The black members were left to fend for themselves. Nathaniel White, who was the key leader, along with Jacob Gilliard and Jack Pierre held prayer meetings. Their efforts helped keep the church members together. Nathaniel White is the great grandfather of Jesse White. Around 1868, the Frierson area began to calm down from the effects of the Civil War and the church was reorganized. At that time, there were around four white members and 46 black members. After the reorganization, white members had church services once a month in Kingston at a school house, and black members had church service across the road (from the white member's school house) in a log cabin. Both groups shared the same white pastor and the one white elder.

In the spring of 1877, a petition was sent to the Red River Presbytery by Elder Jacob Gilliard asking that the "Colored Congregation" be constituted into a church of their own and keep the name Good Hope. The Red River Presbytery granted the petition. In the fall of 1877, Mr. Harrington, a white minister acting as moderator, organized the present Good Hope Presbyterian Church. Nathaniel White, Jacob Gilliard, Jack Pierre, Robert Frierson, and others were present at this meeting.

After this change, the meetings of the church were held at the home of Elder Nathaniel White for a long time. In 1878, the members built a church on the land that today is still owned by Good Hope Presbyterian Church. The first building was a log structure with a mud chimney at one end and a door in the other. Two other buildings were constructed over the years, but on June 1st, 1982, under the leadership and pastorate of Reverend Dr. David L. Jones Sr., a ground-breaking ceremony was held to begin construction of the present brick building.

During the time of the first two buildings, the church did not have pastors or deacons. White ministers were doing the preaching. Sometime in 1879, Reverend Fortune Pierre was ordained and elected as pastor. More elders were elected including Brothers Andrew White Sr. and Jack Gilliard. L.L. Mitchell was elected the first Clerk of Session at this time. Brothers Billy Gillings and Peter Eddins were elected as the first deacons in 1882.

The following ministers were called and ordained to pastor: Reverend Fortune Pierre (see Photo 3), who was born a slave but died a free man, served for 42 years, from 1879 to 1921, with a meager salary of about $60 to $80 per year; Reverend R.L. Williams served for one year; Reverend William C. Bouchelion served for three years; Reverend Dzandira Chiphe served for four years; Reverend Jawell Carr served two terms: four years and three months the first term, and four years and seven months the second term; Reverend J.C. Stull, served three years and six months; Reverend C.F. Tyler served six years; Reverend J.H. White and Reverend A.M. Plant also served; Reverend Dr. David L. Jones Sr. served as pastor for 36 years, and Reverend Jim Freeman, Reverend Aljay Wiggins, and others served as spiritual leaders in the absence of an appointed pastor. The current pastor, as of 2016, is Reverend Harry W. Cooper. Good Hope Presbyterian Church is now over 139 years old. Below is a picture of Reverend Fortune Pierre who was one of the pioneers and visionaries of Good Hope Presbyterian Church.

Photo 3. Reverend Fortune Pierre

It must be reiterated that original members petitioning for their own church wanted to keep the name "Good Hope." Not any kind of hope, but *good* hope. In order to sustain and survive the complexities of the American system, good hope and plenty of faith were needed.

Jesse was a man of few words but decisive action. With deep roots tied to his community and church, he had the innate ability to take care of the business of the church and his home.

We Are Free

Jesse, who was a grandson of slaves, took advantage of his freedom and liberties in our American democracy. It is difficult to know how our ancestors first felt when they were first set free as a people. The free labor of slaves who built this nation was the greatest gift to America. Due to the free labor given, America was able to compete globally in commerce. Merriam-Webster defined democracy as a government by the people; *especially*: rule of the majority. Jesse's ancestors, while enslaved were considered property whose primary purpose was to fulfill the dreams of white entrepreneurs. Like others of African ancestry, Jesse and his family were only partially eligible members of the American states because true freedom did not exist for them; they were intended for lives of servitude. No doubt about it, slavery was a horrible institution within the American democracy. The following poem expresses what Jesse's ancestors felt when they were finally set free from American bondage:

All my life I have worked
All my life I have served
All my life I have been controlled
All my life I have done all that I could with what I had
Now I am free, now I am free
There is a God

The 4th of July was definitely acknowledged within Jesse's household, but the family was well aware of the Emancipation Proclamation, 13th Amendment, segregation, self-reliance and freedom. In addition, Jesse understood the history behind Juneteenth, which pertained to the official date of June 19th, 1865. On this date Major General Gordon Granger landed in Galveston, Texas and proclaimed the war's end and announced that all slaves were free! Unfortunately, this news reached the state Texas two and a half years after President Lincoln's Emancipation Proclamation.

Within Jesse's home, the 4th of July was celebrated with a

combination of acknowledging the American democracy as well as knowing its sad history. Here is another poem from a different perspective of how it must have felt to be free for the first time in America:

Where do we go from here?
I am free but I have deep fear
Strong fear of the unknown
We as a people we are all alone
I will pray, I will focus and use spiritual meditation
The primary solution for freedom is a great education
Starting all over again it will not be easy
Let's move forward and get busy

Jesse knew, as his ancestors did, that the key to success was an education. At one time in our history it was against the law for enslaved blacks to read and write. Jesse was going to make sure his children were educated. Many of Jesse's female siblings were educated at Grambling College. Jesse's father Hezekiah sent several of his daughters off to college. His sons were required to work the farm and possibly take over the family business upon Hezekiah's passing. Jesse always regretted not going to college, particularly since a couple of his sisters had college degrees. Therefore, Jesse made sure all his children, both male and female, attended college.

Deep Ties to DeSoto Parish

Jesse White, the White family, and extended family are deeply tied to DeSoto Parish, Louisiana. None of Jesse's ancestors received their "40 Acres and a Mule." It is unfortunate that our federal government never truly addressed the free labor given by American black slaves. White America in general did not see blacks as equal citizens, but Southern whites were more honest in their refusal to acknowledge what black people had been enslaved to do. It only seems fair to compensate those who were directly descended from slaves for the work they performed while enslaved. If not 40 acres and a mule, how about a free education? Or how about being taught instrumental ways from the state and local government to assist blacks to assimilate into the competitive job market in order to compete with the best Americans? Slaves started at a poor disadvantage after being set free. Or maybe General William Tecumseh Sherman knew this "40 and a mule" concept would be a waste of federal and state money since Congress knew society in general wanted to keep blacks in their place. The idea of 40 acres and mule was no more than a broken promise. This "broken promise" implemented through Special Field Order No. 15 was overturned by President Andrew Johnson (a southern sympathizer) in the fall of 1865 (Gates, et al., 2013).

The oldest known document associated with the White family as well as other black families in DeSoto Parish area has been identified. See Figure 13, the 1867 contract with Freedmen in Frierson / Lakeville, Louisiana.

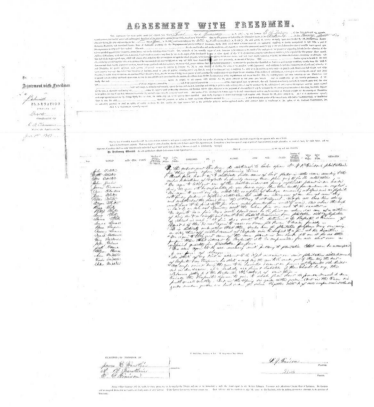

*Figure 13. 1867 contract with Freedmen in Frierson /
Lakeville, Louisiana*

This agreement with freedmen in Lakeville, Louisiana, which
is an area within Frierson near Gravel Point Road, took place
on the Lakeville Plantation on January 1st, 1867 and outlined
rightful employment of previous slaves for the first time by
S.J. Frierson. The full document has been reproduced in the
following paragraphs.

AGREEMENT WITH FREEDMEN

The agreement (in three parts) made and entered into this _First_ day of _January_ A.D. 1867, by and between _S.J. Frierson_ of the first part and the following named persons, hereinafter named and undersigned, Freedmen of the same place, parties hereto of the second part, Witnesseth: That for the purpose of Cultivating the Plantation known as the _Lakeville_ in the _Parish of DeSoto_ aforesaid during the year commencing on the 1ˢᵗ day of _Jan_. A.D. 1867 and terminating on the 31ˢᵗ day of December A.D. 1867, the said parties do hereby mutually agree that the Circular No. 29, Headquarters Bureau Refugees, Freedmen, and Abandoned Lands, State of Louisiana, providing for the Employment and general welfare of Freedmen, Series 1865, all of which is hereto annexed, (or separately supplied) is hereby incorporated in and made a part of this Agreement as fully as if here recited. The said _____ for the consideration and on the conditions and stipulations hereinafter mentioned, agrees to pay to the said Laborers the rates of monthly wages agreed upon and as specified opposite their respective names hereto, and in the following manner to-wit: One twentieth of the monthly wages of such Laborers to be retained in the hands of the employer for the purpose of supporting Schools for the education of the children of Freedmen, to be paid over at the end of each month so much as may then be due, to the Agent of the Freedmen's Bureau or other Agent of the U.S. Government, properly authorized to receive it, to be expended for the purpose above named. One-half of the wages agreed upon, which will remain after deducting the one twentieth set apart for school purposes, to be punctually paid to the laborers during each and every month, reckoning from the day when this Contract commences as aforesaid; and the remaining one-half together

111

with such portion of the one twentieth set apart for Schools as may not have been demanded and paid over previously, at the end of the year. Said _____ further agrees to furnish to the said Laborers and those rightly dependent on them, free of charge, good and sufficient quarters, wholesome food, proper clothing, fuel, and medical attendance; to see the premises thus furnished are kept in a good sanitary condition; to allot from the lands of said Plantation for garden purposes, such portion of ground as may be allowed by Circular No. 29, to each Laborer or Family, the same to be specified in this Agreement, such allotment to include a reasonable use of tools and animals; exact only ten hours per day and no labor whatever on Sunday's, except in cases of positive necessity, and if any labor is excess of ten hours per day is rendered, the same is to be paid for as extra labor; to grant to such laborers one half of each and every Saturday to enable them to cultivate the portions of land allotted to them, also the Fourth of July; to co operate in and encourage the establishment of any School for the education of the children of said Laborers, and to give, free of rent, the use of such piece of ground, not exceeding one-fourth of one acre, as may be most suitable and convenient for the erection of a School house for the accommodation of the neighborhood, and not to interfere with the dwelling-house and other buildings on the Plantation; and finally the said _____ agrees to comply in all respects with Circular No. 29, above referred to and made part hereof. *And in consideration of the* faithful performance of the said _____ of all the obligations assume by _____ and of the punctual payment by _____ of the wages agreed upon as aforesaid, the said Laborers do severally, and each for himself, agree with the said _____ heirs and assigns to faithfully and honestly, and to the best of their skill, knowledge and ability, to perform such ordinary labor as may be necessary for the cultivation of such crops as the employer may see proper to plant for the term as aforesaid; and during the _____ season do agree to work on Saturday afternoons, and Sundays, and at night, whenever in the judgment of the employer it may be necessary for the securing and or preservation of the crops, for which they are to be paid at the rate of one day's labor, and to receive (1/2) one-half ration extra for every six hours' work. Said parties of the second part do further agree to do such extraordinary work as may be necessary on Sundays or night, for the security of Plantations and crops against destruction by storms, floods, fire, or frost, for which they are to be paid as above specified. And finally they agree to observe and comply in all respects with Circular No. 29, above referred to. *And it is furthermore agreed*: That in case the said _____ shall fail, neglect, or refuse to fulfill any of the obligations assumed by _____ or shall furnish said parties of the second part, with bad or insufficient food, or insufficient or unhealthy quarters, or shall be guilty of cruelty to them, be shall besides the legal recourse left to the particular party or parties aggrieved, render their contract liable to annulment at the option of the Assistant Commissioner, &c.

And it is furthermore mutually agreed

That in lieu of monthly wages the said Laborers shall be entitled to and agree to accept the share of the nett profits of carrying on the plantation aforesaid, respectively set opposite their names below. And it is furthermore agreed, That any wages or share of profits, due the said Laborers under this Agreement, shall constitute a first lien upon all crops or parts of crops produced on said plantation or tract of land, by their labor; and no shipment of products shall be made until the duly authorized Agent shall certify that all dues to laborers are paid or satisfactorily arranged.

In Testimony Whereof, the said parties have affixed their names to this Agreement at _____ State of _____ on the day and date aforesaid.

We the undersigned Freedmen do contract to labor upon Dr. G.P. Frierson's plantation's for this year upon the following terms.

1. Each full hand is to cultivate sixteen acres of land planted in cotton & corn according to the wishes & directions of Proprietor the furnishing necessary mules plowed gearing & for its cultivation

2. We agree to take good care of these work animals & all farming implements placed in our hands during the year & to be responsible for all loss or injury done there resulting from carelessness or neglect

3. We agree to work every day with the exception of Sundays commencing at sunrise or forfeit 50 cents for every failure & continue until sunset with an intermission of one hour at noon during cool weather & of two hours from the 15th May to 15th August. And for all loss time during work hours to be fined 20 cents per hour unless prevented from work by rain. And when the crop laid by ox does not require any work the above fines are not to be exacted.

4. We agree to do a fair days work & do it well or be fined as above & in case of a continuance of doing bad or

insufficient work to be liable to dismission from plantation with a forfeiture of interest in crop. A fair days work to be determined by Proprietor & Forman of Squad & if they do not agree to call in some fit person to decide finally.

5. It is distinctly understood that these mules are for plantation purposes & any one using or riding them off without consent of the Proprietor will be subject to a fine at his discretion

6. We agree to take good care of the corn placed in our hands & to use it for no other purpose than that intended by Proprietor & to be responsible for all used over a sufficient quantity for plantation purposes

7. We also agree to do all necessary work pertaining to plantation that can be accomplished by us free of charge

8. No stock of any kind is allowed to be kept or raised on said plantation without consent of Proprietor & any trespass on his stock or crop during the year to be made good by thou doing the deed

9. All crops raised during the year to be harvested & grown on premises of Proprietor to be divided out in due season, after deducting all fines & liabilities if then should be any, the Laborer getting ½ & the Proprietor the other ½ of said fines. Finally the Proprietor agrees to give to each full hand 3 ½ pounds meat & one pick meal weekly. And in the Spring six yards cotton goods. And in the Fall six yards woolen goods, one hat & one pair of shoes together with 1/3 of all crops raised & harvested.

T. Fitzwilliam, Stationer & Printer 76 Camp Street, New Orleans

EXECUTED IN PRESENCE OF

JAMES E FRANKLIN APPROVED.   S.J. Frierson
W B FRANKLIN   PLANTER.
T G FRIERSON   DeSoto
                                             PARISH.

NOTE --- This Contract will be made in three parts, one to be kept by the Planter, and two to be forwarded through the Local Agent to the Bureau Refugees, Freedmen and Abandoned Lands, State of Louisiana. No Contract will be accepted which does not contain the family name of each Laborer. If the Laborer has not one he must assume one. Each Laborer will be required to sign his name to this Contract, either by making his mark or otherwise in the presence of Witnesses.

1. John Allston
2. Bette Allston
3. Peter Allston
4. John Guion
5. James Freeman
6. Gacer Flanders
7. Jesse White
8. Tiller White
9. Edgar White
10. Bicy White
11. Phillip White
12. Nancy White
13. Dorcus White
14. Isaac Small
15. Bess Small

16. Cassar Small
17. Fany Caldwell
18. John Holmes
19. Jack Holmes
20. Flora Holmes
21. Sam Midleton
22. Francis Midleton
23. Amelia Midleton

Our family has deep ties to this document. It clearly defines the criteria by which each employed worker is required to abide, and which Dr. George P. Frierson was instrumental is compiling. Please note that Jesse White and Tiller White are husband and wife. In addition, they were the paternal grandparents of Jesse White. Phillip White is the father of both Nancy White and Dorcus White. In addition, Phillip White is the uncle of Jesse White, who is the seventh name listed within the freedmen agreement. Phillip White was the first Sunday School Superintendent at Good Hope Presbyterian Church. Phillip was the younger brother of Nathaniel White. Both brothers took the long wagon trail ride from South Carolina to Alabama and then to DeSoto Parish as slaves within their lifetimes with the Frierson family. Phillip White would not purchase land until the year 1885, approximately 18 years after the establishment of the agreement with the freedmen. Phillip White was the first direct descendant of the White family to purchase land: approximately 100 acres for $324.00 in DeSoto Parish. Figure 14 is a copy of the first land purchase between St. Julian Frierson and Phillip White.

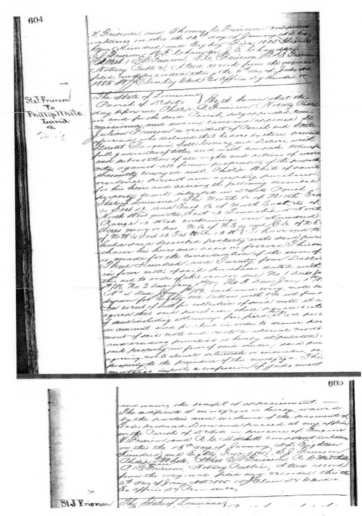

Figure 14. Copy of the first land purchase between St. Julian Frierson and Phillip White

The land purchase between Frierson and White occurred on January 6th, 1885.

It has not been confirmed thus far if the James Freeman who is listed at number five in the agreement is the grandfather of Erma Freeman White's father, Papa James Freeman, who did not live far from the Lakeville area in Kingston. Both Jesse White (# 7) and Edgar White (# 9) are the sons of Nathaniel White. Sam Midleton, Amelia Midleton, Peter Allston, John Holmes, Fany Caldwell, Jesse White, Tiller White, and Edgar White were all the original 1877 charter members of Good Hope Presbyterian Church.

Photo 4. Lakeville Plantation area in the year 2016

Since the Freedmen Agreement, not much has physically changed in Lakeville over the last 150 years. Lakeville is still rural and family oriented. Some of the descendants of the people listed in the Freedmen Agreement still reside in Frierson although not in Lakeville.

Happy Birthday, Nathaniel

The oldest recorded patriarch of the White family linked to Jesse White is his great grandfather Nathaniel White, who was born in 1816 in the state of South Carolina. Currently it is not known how the family inherited the last name White, but sometime between 1836 and 1838, Nathaniel moved to Lowndes County, Alabama with Dr. George P. Frierson and family. Charlotte (Caldwell) White was also born in South Carolina in 1819. It is not known if Charlotte took the 500-mile wagon trail ride with Nathaniel to Alabama, but they became husband and wife while in Lowndes County. They had six children, beginning in 1845, with the birth of their son Jesse, who was born in Lowndes County, Alabama. Their remaining children—Edgar White, Andrew White, Bass White, Hager White (female), and Ben White—were born in DeSoto Parish, Louisiana.

Between 1850 and 1851, Dr. Frierson moved from Lowndes County, Alabama to DeSoto Parish, Louisiana with his family along with his black slaves. The automobile still hadn't been invented yet and the 480-mile journey to DeSoto Parish took a few weeks. With God's grace, Jesse White and Tillah Caldwell married and raised a family in Louisiana. Tillah was born in 1846 in Lowndes County, Alabama. She and Jesse had seven children: Jenny, Dinah, George, Ed, James Henry, Hezekiah, and Dicy, who was about a year old when Jesse White died, between 1878 and 1880. It had to be tough on Tillah to be widowed with seven children. Hezekiah was not older than three years old when his father Jesse died.

With life taking its toll and Father Time and Mother Nature playing their part, the two eldest family members passed away. One of the original founders of Good Hope Presbyterian Church, Nathaniel White, died on May 18th,

1884. His lovely wife Charlotte died on October 18th, 1898. Both are buried at Good Hope Presbyterian Church in what is known today as the old cemetery.

Farming was a big part of life during those times. It was common to work the fields and share crop on the lands of previous owners. The farmer's spouse played a major role in the planting and harvesting of crops, too. Hezekiah White Sr. was a good farmer. Hezekiah was blessed to meet Emma Edward, who was from the Gloster, Louisiana area, and he married her in 1901. They had five children, one of whom was a son that was called home to be with the Lord as a child. The remaining four were Tillah, Phyllis, Elsie, and Hezekiah, Jr. Emma Edward White came from a prosperous, land-owning family. She inherited her parents' land and that inheritance was instrumental in the foundation of White family's early financial growth. Hezekiah White Sr., was known as a shrewd businessman, and he made several great business decisions that led to more capital and more prosperity for his family.

Hezekiah White, Sr. purchased approximately 80 acres of land from the Frierson brothers on December 9th, 1902 for $123.00. Figure 15 is an image of the record of that purchase, which was one of several wise transactions made by Hezekiah White, Sr.

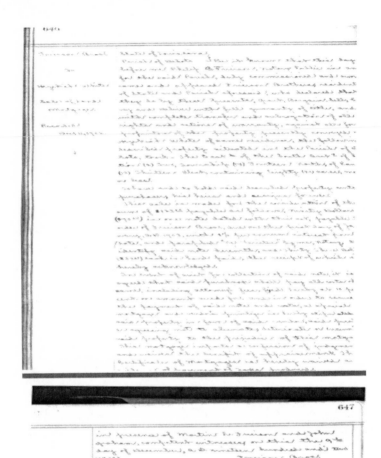

Figure 15. Record of land purchased by Hezekiah White, Sr.

Hezekiah and Emma were blessed. Then a sad event occurred. On August 26, 1910 Emma passed away, leaving Hezekiah with four children and no mother to assist in their rearing.

Fortunately, Hezekiah remarried on January 16th, 1913

to his second wife, Alfair Lee Jones White. They had six children together: Patsy, Jesse, Gennah, Edith, and Nehemiah. The sixth child, a daughter, was called home to be with the Lord as a child.

After years of hard work, Hezekiah became a successful self-employed businessman with a thriving farming business. Today, he would be called a "self-made" man. He had several employees and an abundance of equipment. He paid taxes and he purchased and sold more land. He was well-respected in the community. If someone within a community needed a reference, a positive word from Hezekiah White Sr. would just about guarantee his or her acceptance. His word and opinion were respected within the community by all races. In the late 1920s, 1930s, and 1940s, at his peak, Hezekiah's gross wages for his business were in the $100,000 range. According to DollarTimes.com (2016), with an annual inflation rate of 3.79% and total inflation of 1589.46%, that amount is equivalent to more than $1,689,464.28 in gross business earnings.

In life, all things come to an end. Elder Hezekiah White Sr. was called to the Lord on April 29, 1967 at the age of 90. His wife Alfair would live 21 years after his passing. She died on May 20, 1988 at the age of 98.

Approximately 200 years after Nathaniel White and Charlotte Caldwell White began building a legacy, their descendants have maintained their ancestors' dynasty. Nathaniel's descendants are God-fearing, and an extremely high percentage of high school graduates, college graduates, accountants, doctors, lawyers, preachers, inventors, manufacturers, and educators. Nathaniel and Charlotte White have over 500 descendants of whom they would be proud. Hezekiah White Sr., Emma Edward White, and Alfair Lee Jones White have over 250 descendants.

God works in mysterious ways and His blessings are

plentiful. The White family has come a long way by faith. Recently, Hezekiah White Sr.'s mother's grave was found at the current grave site of Good Hope Presbyterian Church. The family is blessed with the recent rediscovery, shown in Photo 5.

Photo 5. Mother Tiller White (1846–Feb. 6, 1917)
"She hath done what she could."

Happy 200th birthday, Nathaniel. Without the sacrifices of Nathaniel and the other brave ancestors, none of their descendants' achievements could have been possible.

Creation

Nathaniel White beget Jesse White, who beget Hezekiah White, who beget Jesse White, who beget Hezekiah White III, who beget Dexter White & Darrell White, which is six generations of genetic ties of father to son, all of whom share the DNA haplogroup[1] E1b1a8a1[2] from the paternal Y chromosome. The DNA of Jesse White's third child, Hezekiah White III, was used to determine the genetic ties globally. Figure 16 is a graph that summarizes the DNA details mentioned for Jesse's paternal line genetic makeup:

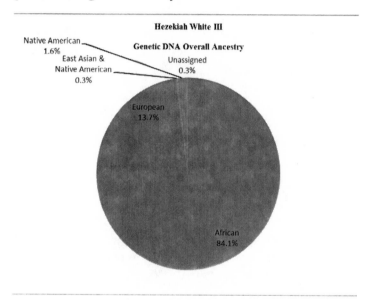

Hezekiah White III

Genetic DNA Overall Ancestry

Native American 1.6%

East Asian & Native American 0.3%

Unassigned 0.3%

European 13.7%

African 84.1%

Figure 16. Summary of the DNA details for Jesse White's paternal genetic makeup

The DNA of Hezekiah White III revealed 84.0% Sub-Saharan

---

1   According to Estes (2013), "Think of a haplogroup as an ancestral clan, a large family…."

2   According to Pour, et al. (2012), "All haplogroups within E1b1a were observed in the Bantu Homeland, West-Central Africa, East Africa and Ghana, whereas haplogroup E1b1a8a1a, although present in the Bantu Homeland and East Africa, was not observed in either Ghana or West-Central Africa."

African ancestry, which includes 78.7% West African ancestry. In addition, Hezekiah's DNA shows 13.7% European ancestry, which includes 5.9% British & Irish, 5.2% Northwestern European, 0.9% Southern European, and 1.7% broadly European. It was always believed that the family had some Native American blood ties and the DNA shows approximately 2% Native American ancestry.

Hezekiah White III's DNA results did show genetic ties in both Upper Guinea and Lower (or Maritime) Guinea in Africa. Without a doubt, over the last 300 years our paternal ancestors came from the west coast of Africa, and it has been determined that Jesse's lineage most closely matches that of people found in the Lower Guinea region. This region runs from the eastern Ivory Coast to western Cameroon. It includes three sub-regions linked to the ports described in middle passage shipping records. These regions are the Gold Coast, the Bight of Benin, and the Bight of Biafra. Jesse's Y-DNA was also found in the Senegambia, Sierra Leone and Liberia region of West Africa. Hezekiah White III paternal haplogroup (E1b1a8a1*) reaches levels of up to 90% among the Mandingo and Yoruba people of western Africa (O'Toole, 2015). The Jesse White paternal family geographic ship and road map begins in Lower Guinea in West Africa to South Carolina to Lowndes County, Alabama, and then on to DeSoto Parish, Louisiana.

Although currently we do not know the names of Nathaniel's mother and father, we know they both were in South Carolina prior to 1816 since Nathaniel White was born there. Figure 17 is a breakdown of the percentage of the slaves imported from 1763 to 1807 to the state of South Carolina.

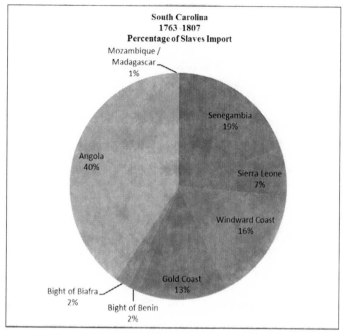

Figure 17. Percentage of the slaves imported from 1763 to 1807 to South Carolina

Slaves transported on ships during the transatlantic slave trade between 1763 and 1807 who disembarked in South Carolina had a 40% chance of coming from Angola, 19% chance of coming from Senegambia, 16% chance of coming from the Windward Coast (present-day Liberia and Côte d'Ivoire (Ivory Coast)), 13% chance of coming from the Gold Coast (present-day Ghana), 7% chance of coming from Sierra Leone, 2% chance of coming from the Bight of Biafra, 2% chance of coming from the Bight of Benin, and a 1% chance of coming from Mozambique and Madagascar. It should be noted that of all the West African countries, Hezekiah White III's DNA appeared to have had the strongest genetic ties to Ghana.

The family will never know if Nathaniel parents' siblings or parents' first cousins died during the transatlantic slave voyage, since it is known that the bodies of dead slaves were just tossed into the Atlantic Ocean. The inhumane environment of those slave ships was no place for the ill or weak. Only the strong survived the transatlantic slave trade. The African Americans who live today in America come from the strong survivors of an inhumane, segregated and unfair system.

Homecoming

As a husband and father, Jesse White worked a combination of jobs. He was a farmer, bus driver, and laborer at the Olin Creosote Plant. As an elder of the church, Jesse White studied, taught, and understood the Bible intimately. As the leader of his family, Jesse used tough love to rear his twelve children, all of whom were taught to work hard and to be responsible.

As a grandfather, Jesse was warm and loving, and required every grandchild to call him "Big Daddy." Jesse taught several of his older grandchildren some of the basic skills of farming. For example, he taught them how to remove kernels of corn from the cob quickly, so that those kernels could be used to feed the chickens. In addition, he taught them when and how to collect their own fresh eggs from the farm's chickens for breakfast.

A good family name was important to Jesse. Although he was known for his soft-spoken demeanor, he was also known as a person who meant exactly what he said. Jesse was a very hard working man and his actions spoke much louder than his words. Driven by thankfulness, faith and hope, the patriarch of the family died of cancer on February 15, 1975. He was 59 years old. His tombstone speaks to the core of who

Jesse White was. It reads: *I have done my best in the race, I have run the full distance, I have kept the faith.*

In heaven an angel is no one in particular.
George Bernard Shaw

DeSoto Parish Community

In regards to municipalities and communities, the Louisiana state government in 2016 listed the following information about DeSoto Parish: the only city was Mansfield; the towns were Keachi, Logansport, and Stonewall; the villages were Grand Cane, Longstreet, South Mansfield, and Stanley; and the unincorporated communities were Frierson and Kingston. It has been said that if you want to get married and you live in DeSoto Parish, it is probably best to leave the area for if you trace far enough back your love interest could possibly be a distant cousin. In an adventurous effort, Figure 18 is a breakdown of surnames of families related to descendants of Nathaniel and Charlotte White as well as the Freeman, the Green and the Winters family line.

Line Number	Erma Freeman	Willie Green	Senie Winters	Jesse White
1	Murray	Carroll	Brown	Alexander
2	Murry	Dunn	Bennett	Anderson
3	Norris	Scott	Collins	Caldwell
4	Preston	Williams	Edwards	Clinton
5	Ware		Douglas	Holmes
6			Hart	Jones
7			Hill	Pierre
8			Nelson	Whited
9			Pennywell	
10			Powers	

Figure 18. Surnames of Freeman, Green, Winters and
White Family Descendants

Figure 18 identifies specific surnames that are related by each of my four grandparents. For example, Erma Freeman is related to the Murrays, Prestons and the Wares, just to name a few. Willie Green is related to the Carrolls and the Scotts; Senie Winters is related to the Browns and the Pennywells; and Jesse White is related to the Caldwells and Pierres, etc. It's a family affair.

The black community of DeSoto Parish is erudite and esoteric. Within their community are colloquial expressions. For example, if one said "*Fan the gnats*," he or she meant "*Whoop your ass.*" In this case "whoop" means "whip." Also, when one said "*What you know good?*" he or she means "*What can you tell me today that is good?*" The word "*river*" was used in a unique way. In DeSoto Parish community, the statement "*I am going to the River,*" "*Meet me at the River,*" or "*Go down by the River*" means "*I am going to the Plantation,*" "*Meet me at the Plantation*" or "*Go down by the Plantation,*" respectively. Some of the plantations located in the Frierson area were the Frierson Plantation, Lakeville Plantation, Guy Plantation, Means Plantation, Odom Plantation, Roach Plantation, Scott Plantation and the Thickpin Plantation.

The term reckon, which means to consider, is commonly used in the area, too. For example, one would say "you reckon that corn planted will harvest this season?" Yonder was a popular and common word in the area during the late 20th century. It was pronounced "yonda." One might say something similar to "go over yonda and get me some of that wood for the stove."

Locals did not need a clock to tell time. They used the position of the sun during daylight hours. The position of a person's shadow during those hours helped him or her determine the time. If the sun was directly over one's head, it was noon time. Although locals typically ate three meals a day, they did not call those meals breakfast, lunch and dinner. They called those meals breakfast, dinner, and supper. Dinner was held typically around noon time and supper, served in the evening, was the last meal of the day.

As is the case in most regions of the United States, DeSoto Parish has its own dialect. Figure 19 is a list of other colloquial expressions.

Word	Pronounced	Definition / Contemporary Pronunciation	Used in a Sentence
buya	bī ̄ ya	bayou	Let's go over to the "buya" and catch some fish.
chair	chār'	here	Bring it "chair" and not over yonda.
chillens	chil' lenz	children	How many "chillens" do you have?
comear	kum mir	come here	Young man, "comear" right now!
dare	dār	there	"dare" he or "dare" he is
dat	dāt	that	Please give me "dat"
day	dā	they	"day" went over there
dees	dēs	these	"dees" are mine
den	den	then	"den" they wanted more biscuits
dim	dim'	them	"dim" pants are mine on the clothes line
dis	dis	this	"dis" is mine
dose	dōs	those	"dose" are my socks
ef	əf	if	"ef" you give me money, we can go
fetch	fech	to bring	Go "fetch" me that shovel
fina	fin' a	getting ready to	I "fina" go to the kitchen
garry	gār'ē	porch	Go sit on the "garry"
gimme	gim' ē	give me	please "gimme" some candy
git	git	get	Please "git" me a hammer
gonna	gôn' ə	going to	I am "gonna" win this race
hockey	hok'ē	do do	Go to the outhouse (bathroom) and "hockey"
jew	jū	you	"jew" never gave me the correct amount.
kinfolk	kin' fōk	family	Here comes your "kinfolk".
mournen	mōr'nin	morning	Good "mournen" momma!
naw	nô	no	"naw", I am not doing nothing
nun	nun	none	I don't have "nun"
nutin	nut' en	nothing	Believe "nutin" you hear regarding that
om	om'	I am	"om" going to the store
oughta	ôt' a	should do	You "oughta" spend less money
pute	pūt	fart	I have to "pute"
sho nuf	shō nuf'	correct or right	"sho nuf", that is amazing he ran so fast
story	stôr'ē	lie	Please do not "story" to me
sumin	sum' en	something	You got "sumin"
toofis	tūf' is	teeth	She lost a lot of her "toofis"
wa	wô	were	You "wa" not there at the same time as I
wanna	won' ə	want to	I "wanna" cook that cat fish by the bayou
wid	wid'	with	I am going "wid" you
whicha way	hwich'ə wā	direction	I was wondering "whicha way" you were going
years	yirs	ears	Clean your years
yesum	yes' um	yes mam	"yesum", I agree with you
yo	yō	your	I will whip "yo" butt

Figure 19.Sampling of colloquial expressions used in DeSoto Parish

Acknowledgements and References

The research was compiled with the assistance of the following organizations and people:

Good Hope Presbyterian Church records and members
National Archives and Records Association (NARA)
Ella Deloise Green White
Elizabeth Green Mitchell
Mackie Lee White Carter
Ophelia Caldwell Stull
Hezekiah White III
Ralph White
Goldie Murray
Jeremiah Jobe White Sr.
Lossie May White Gibson
Velberly Nelson Rodriquez
Willie James White
Cassandra Green Rice
African DNA
23 and Me
Lugene Green
Sandra Oten
Ancestry.com
LSU-Shreveport Archives and Special Collections
Noel Memorial Library
Ruby Green Brown
Jeanette Clark
Leeman Green

Memoirs of Edith Chiphe

Shreve Memorial Library's Genealogy Department located at the Broadmoor Branch

H.K. White Sr. Family Reunion Records

Jesse & Erma White Family Reunion Records

Dorothy White

Wikipedia

Veronica White Davis and the DeSoto Parish Courthouse

I would like to give a special thank you to my editors, Lauren Jones and Jennifer Bruyns, for their hard work in helping to prepare my book for publication.

Additional References

Ambler, Rex (1989). Gandhi's concept of truth. In J. Hick, L. Hempel, J. C. Dillman, J. D. Maguire, & C. E Wright, Eds. (1989). *Gandhi's Significance for Today: The Elusive Legacy* (pp. 90-108). New York: St. Martin's Press.

Alkire, S. & Newell, E. (2005). What can one person do? Faith to heal a broken world. New York: Church Publishing, Incorporated.

Armstrong, April C. (2015). Mudd Manuscript Library Blog. Retrievedfromhttps://blogs.princeton.edu/mudd/201505/african-americans-and-princeton-university/

Ash, Stephen V., et al. Reconstruction. *World Book Encyclopedia. 2012 ed.*

Berg, A. Scott (1985). *Wilson.* New York: Penguin Group.

Berlatsky, Noah (2010). America's Prisons Opposing Viewpoints. USA: Greenhaven Press.

Berlin, Ira (2010). The Making of African America The Four Great Migrations. USA: Penguin Group.

Boothe, Demico (2007). Why Are So Many Black Men in Prison? USA: Full Surface Publishing.

Cooper, Belinda, et al. Reparations. *World Book Encyclopedia. 2012 ed.*

Countries and Their Cultures (2015). Culture of Guinea: Demography. Retrieved from http://www.everyculture.com/Ge-It/Guinea.html

Dollar Times (2016). Retrieved from http://www.dollartimes.com/inflation/inflation.php?amount=100000&year=1940.

Estes, R. (January 24, 2013). What is a haplogroup? [Web log post]. Retrieved from http://dna-explained.com/2013/01/24/what-is-a-haplogroup/

Esty, Amos (2012). Plessy v. Ferguson. USA: Morgan Reynolds Publishing, Inc.

Ethnologue (2015). Languages of the world: Guinea. Retrieved from http://www.ethnologue.com/country/GN

Faux, Jeff (2013). NAFTA's Impact on U.S. Workers. *Economic Policy Institute*. Retrieved from http://www.epi.org/blog/naftas-impact-workers/.

Ford, Richard (2011). Rights Gone Wrong How Law Corrupts the Struggle for Equality. New York: Farrar, Straus and Giroux.

Gable, John A., et al. "Theodore Roosevelt" *World Book Encyclopedia. 2012 ed.*

Gates, H. L. (2013). The Truth Behind '40 Acres and a Mule' [Blog post] Retrieved from http://www.theroot.com/articles/history/2013/01/40_acres_and_a_mule_promise_to_slaves_the_real_story/3/

Gates, H. L. & Garceau, Z. (2015, November 7). How did my enslaved kin get to Va. from Madagascar? [Blog post] Retrieved from http://www.theroot.com/articles/history/2015/11/tracing_slaves_brought_from_madagascar_to_va.html

Hamby, Alonzo L., et al. "Harry S. Truman" *World Book Encyclopedia. 2012 ed.*

Ivers, Greg. Plessy v. Ferguson. *World Book Encyclopedia. 2012 ed.*

Keith, LeeAnna (2008). The Colfax Massacre. New York: Oxford University Press, Inc.

Library of Congress (2010). The African American mosaic: Colonization. Retrieved from https://www.loc.gov/exhibits/african/afam002.html

Maney, Patrick J., et al. "Franklin Delano Roosevelt" *World Book Encyclopedia. 2012 ed.*

Miller, Merle (1981). Lyndon An Oral Biography. New York:

G.P. Putnam's Sons.

Miller, Nathan (1992), et al. Theodore Roosevelt, A Life. New York: William Morrow & Company

Morgan, Ted (1985). 'FDR A Biography'. New York: Simon and Schuster.

Mulder, John M., et al. "Woodrow Wilson" *World Book Encyclopedia. 2012 ed.*

Nelson, David Eric (2009). Racial Profiling Opposing Viewpoints. USA: Greenhaven Press.

Office of Equal Opportunity and Diversity (2015). A brief history of affirmative action. Retrieved from http://www.oeod.uci.edu/aa.html

O'Toole, T. E. (2015). Guinea. *Encyclopedia Britannica.* Retrieved from http://www.britannica.com/place/Guinea.

Our Africa (2015). Senegal: People and culture: Ancient ancestry. Retrieved from http://www.our-africa.org/senegal/people-culture

Pour, N. A., Plaster, C. A., & Bradman, N. (2012). Evidence from Y-chromosome analysis for a late exclusively eastern expansion of the Bantu-speaking people. *European Journal of Human Genetics (2013) 21*, 423–429. doi:10.1038/ejhg.2012.176. Published online 15 August 2012

Racism Review (2014). White Women and Affirmative Action: Prime Beneficiaries and opponents. Retrieved from http://www.racismreview.com/blog/2014/03/11/white-women-affirmative-action/

Reeves, Thomas C. (1991). A Question of Character A Life of John F. Kennedy. New York: The Free Press.

Schafer, Judith (1997), et al., The Louisiana Purchase Bicentennial Series in Louisiana History, Volume XIII An Uncommon Experience Law and Judicial Institutions in Louisiana 1803 – 2003. Louisiana: The Centers of Louisiana Studies

Schott, Jeffrey J. "North American Free Trade Agreement (NAFTA)" *World Book Encyclopedia. 2012 ed.*

Shabazz, Ilyasah (2002), et al., Growing Up X. New York: One World, Ballantine Publishing Group

Stiglitz, Joseph E. (2012). The Price of Inequality. New York: W. W. Norton & Company, Inc.

Theodore Roosevelt: An American Lion (2003). Directed by David De Vries. USA, A & E Television Networks. [Film]

Thomas, G. S. (2008). Advice from the presidents: The student's guide to reaching the top in business and politics. Westport, CT: Greenwood Press.

Time (2013). Affirmative Action Has Helped White Women More Than Anyone. Retrieved from http://ideas.time.com/2013/06/17/affirmative-action-has-helped-white-women-more-than-anyone/

US Library of Congress. Primary documents in American history. Retrieved from https://www.loc.gov/rr/program/bib/ourdocs/13thamendment.html)

Wicker, Tom (2002). Dwight D. Eisenhower. New York: Henry Holt and Company.

Winbush, Raymond A. (2003), et al. Should America Pay? Slavery and the Raging Debate on Reparations. New York: HarperCollins Publishers, Inc.

Index

CPSIA information can be obtained
at www.ICGtesting.com
Printed in the USA
LVOW11s1408140717
541283LV00001B/2/P